"After pastoring a church for fifteen yea[rs] and encouraging to read. It reminded me his shepherds to do. I highly recommend ...this book for any pastor, whether you're just starting out, or have been faithfully shepherding for decades."

—*Matt Carter, pastor of preaching and vision, Austin Stone Community Church*

"Nothing is more important to the church today than to have a clear view of the role of the pastor, who is the 'undershepherd' of the congregation. And nothing is more important to the pastor/shepherd than to know what God's Word declares about his assignment. The pattern for the shepherd is the Great Shepherd, our Lord Jesus Christ. The role is vital and demanding. The writer of Hebrews concludes in 13:17 that the shepherd must 'give account' to God. James reminds us that he will face 'a stricter judgment' (3:1). The shepherd does not choose to be a shepherd; he is appointed by God to be a shepherd. He is not a hired hand, but a divinely selected leader who loves the sheep and gives his life to them. These pages clearly reveal that the shepherd has a high calling, an enormous responsibility, a demanding holiness of life, and a compassionate ministry given to him on behalf of the church. He is always guided by the example of our Lord Jesus Christ and faithfulness to the sufficiency and complete trustworthiness of God's Word."

—*Jimmy Draper, president emeritus, LifeWay Christian Resources of the Southern Baptist Convention*

"After more than twenty-five years of pastoring, I am convinced that ministry is not for the faint of heart. The Bible calls the pastor a shepherd for a reason— his life is devoted to caring for sheep—and sheep can be messy. Pastors can be messy too. Pastoring well means knowing how to lead well and leading well requires a biblical understanding of what God expects from His shepherds. *Pastoral Ministry* was written for such a purpose. Each chapter will open your eyes to both who God expects pastors to be and what God expects pastors to do. It's more than a 'how to' book; it's a 'who am I' book. Read this and you will gain valuable insights about how to pastor your people, but even greater, you will also be challenged to look within your own heart to consider how God is pastoring you."

—*Mark A. Howell, senior pastor, Hunters Glen Baptist Church*

"The high calling of a pastor is to shepherd the people of God with the Word of God for the glory of God. Indeed, pastors are accountable before God for their stewardship of this high calling. For this reason, I pray that the Lord will bless this book to help encourage and equip pastors to be the shepherds God has called them to be."

—*David Platt, president, the International Mission Board of the Southern Baptist Convention*

PASTORAL
MINISTRY

PASTORAL MINISTRY

The Ministry of a Shepherd

Deron J. Biles

Editor

Series Editors:

Paige Patterson & Jason G. Duesing

A TREASURY OF BAPTIST THEOLOGY

ACADEMIC

NASHVILLE, TENNESSEE

Pastoral Ministry
Copyright © 2017 by Deron J. Biles
Published by B&H Academic
Nashville, Tennessee

ISBN: 978-1-4627-5102-0

Dewey Decimal Classification: 253

Subject Heading: CLERGY \ PASTORAL THEOLOGY \ BIBLE. O.T.
EZEKIEL 34 -- STUDY AND TEACHING

Printed in the United States of America
1 2 3 4 5 6 7 8 9 10 VP 22 21 20 19 18 17

Contents

Dedication

To those who faithfully serve His sheep and
to those faithful shepherds
who look like the Shepherd and
smell like the sheep

Acknowledgments

I am profoundly grateful to my parents, who consistently modeled for me the ministry of a shepherd and the incalculable worth of a faithful shepherd's wife. My father was my first shepherd and has been my lifelong mentor. The words I have written are mine, but the thoughts were first his.

I am grateful to my wife, Jaye, who dared to take this journey with me and has encouraged me at every step. She is a blessing of the Lord to me. She makes me want to be when I preach what she is when she sings. The Lord has blessed us with Josh, Tim, Jon, and Dave; and now KariAnn, Alissa, Kelsey, and Genesis.

I wish to express my appreciation to Dr. and Mrs. Patterson, who have unfailingly modeled the combination of courageous leadership and compassionate care. I'm grateful to Dr. Patterson for the initial support and clarity he gave for this book as well as his vision for this series, and to Mrs. Patterson for the persistent momentum and enthusiasm she has provided, without which this project may never have begun. Thank you for giving me the opportunity to contribute to this series as well as serve with you at Southwestern. I also want to thank Jason Duesing, the coeditor of this series, for his insightful advice and support.

I am thankful for the eight men who have contributed chapters to this book: Paige Patterson, David Allen, Dale Johnson, Malcolm Yarnell, Tommy Kiker, Matt Queen, Fred Luter, and Stephen Rummage. I'm grateful for your insights, your encouragement, and for modeling what you preach.

Finally, I want to express my appreciation to B&H for the invaluable assistance with this book and for the investment in this series; and especially to Renée Chavez, Audrey Greeson, and Jennifer Day.

Abbreviations

AB	Anchor Bible Series
ABD	*The Anchor Bible Dictionary*
BAGD	*A Greek–English Lexicon of the New Testament and Other Early Christian Literature,* 2nd ed., ed. Walter Bauer, trans. William F. Arndt, F. Wilbur Gingrich, and Frederick W. Daner (Chicago: University of Chicago Press, 1979)
BDB	*The Brown-Driver-Briggs Hebrew and English Lexicon*, by Francis Brown, S. R. Driver, and Charles A. Briggs (Boston: Houghton, Mifflin, and Co., 1906; reprint, Peabody, MA: Hendrickson, 1996)
BDBG	*The New Brown-Driver-Briggs-Gesenius Hebrew and English Lexicon*
BECNT	Baker Exegetical Commentary on the New Testament
BibSac	*Bibliotheca Sacra*
BBR	*Bulletin for Biblical Research*
BST	The Bible Speaks Today Series

JCR	*Journal of Communication and Religion*
JRL	*Journal of Religious Leadership*
NAC	The New American Commentary
NICNT	The New International Commentary on the New Testament
NICOT	The New International Commentary on the Old Testament
NIDOTTE	*New International Dictionary of Old Testament Theology and Exegesis*
NIVAC	NIV Application Commentary
NPNF[2]	*A Selected Library of the Nicene and Post-Nicene Fathers of the Christian Church, vol. 2*
SBL	Society of Biblical Literature
TDNT	*Theological Dictionary of the New Testament*
TDOT	*Theological Dictionary of the Old Testament*
TLOT	*Theological Lexicon of the Old Testament*
TWOT	*Theological Wordbook of the Old Testament*
WBC	Word Biblical Commentary
WUNT	Wissenschaftliche Untersuchungen zum Neuen Testament
ZAW	*Zeitschrift für die alttestamentliche Wissenschaft*

Contributors

Editor

Deron J. Biles, professor of pastoral ministries and preaching, and director of professional doctoral studies, School of Theology and Preaching, Southwestern Baptist Theological Seminary

Contributors

David L. Allen, dean of the School of Preaching, Distinguished Professor of Preaching, director of the Southwestern Center for Expository Preaching, and George W. Truett Chair of Ministry, Southwestern Baptist Theological Seminary

T. Dale Johnson Jr., assistant professor of biblical counseling and chair of the biblical counseling division, Southwestern Baptist Theological Seminary

Tommy Kiker, associate professor of pastoral theology, James T. Draper Jr. Chair of Pastoral Ministry, and chair of the pastoral ministry department, Southwestern Baptist Theological Seminary

Fred Luter Jr., senior pastor, Franklin Avenue Baptist Church, and former president of the Southern Baptist Convention

Paige Patterson, president, Southwestern Baptist Theological Seminary, and former president of the Southern Baptist Convention

Matt Queen, L. R. Scarborough Chair of Evangelism ("Chair of Fire"), associate professor of evangelism and associate dean for doctoral programs, Southwestern Baptist Theological Seminary

Stephen Rummage, senior pastor, Bell Shoals Baptist Church; chairman, the Southern Baptist Convention Executive Committee; and president, the Florida Baptist State Convention

Malcolm B. Yarnell III, research professor of systematic theology, director of the Oxford Study Program, and director of the Center for Theological Research, Southwestern Baptist Theological Seminary

A Treasury of Baptist Theology

B aptists have always been grateful for the contributions of great Christians from every era. Where would we be without Athanasius's *The Incarnation of the Son of God,* Augustine's *Confessions*, or the multiplied books of the Reformers who laid the foundations for the Reformation? And as much as we look forward to the return of Christ and a true ecumenism, adjudicated by none other than the Lord from heaven, we must until then be faithful in the expression of the truth as we know it.

The *Treasury of Baptist Theology* represents an effort to do exactly that. This series of more than 30 volumes written by notable Baptist theologians from a number of different institutions and churches reflects the understanding of holy Scripture as Baptists have grasped it. There is diversity among authors, including Asian, German, and French theologians, as well as several Baptist women. Each author is writing from a distinctively Baptist perspective.

As you begin to read these volumes, our prayer to God is that He will use them to encourage faithfulness from all in delivering the New Testament witness to our own era. The concept of a believer's church—that is, a church made up of only twice-born men and women who have witnessed their faith through the covenant of believer's baptism and who have committed themselves wholly to the fulfillment of the Great Commission as given by our Lord in Matthew 28:18–20—will hopefully incline the hearts of all to the Savior and to His program of witness to the nations. Along the way, the plea for religious liberty will also be made apparent, together with the teachings on those doctrines where there is agreement across denominational lines, such as Christology, the Trinity, and other significant foundational doctrines. Volumes on evangelism, apologetics, and God's purposes for the home will also be among those coming from this series.

So begin your journey with us, and hear the significant witness of today's Baptist theologians. And may God help us to embrace these doctrines with the same thoroughness and commitment as those in the generations who have gone before.

Paige Patterson, President
Southwestern Baptist Theological Seminary
Fort Worth, Texas

CHAPTER 1

Introduction: The Ministry of a Shepherd

Deron J. Biles

God, in His grace, called me to be a pastor. It is a calling from which I have never recovered. I remember when God first called me as a 12-year-old boy. I recall walking down the aisle and taking the hand of my pastor, who was also my father, and sharing with him that God had called me to full-time ministry.

Not until a few years later as a 19-year-old pastor of a small church in central Texas did I begin to realize that, despite having been reared in the home of a pastor, I did not really know what a pastor was supposed to do. Three decades later, I am still learning. During that time, I have had the privilege of serving as a pastor, working with pastors at a state convention, and now training pastors at a seminary.

Being a pastor is an audacious calling. It is at once a remarkable privilege and an unaccomplishable task. Imagine the grace of God to call men to be His servants. What a wonderful privilege we have been given! Yet, the task is so great, who can be worthy? Just as the Lamb alone is worthy to loose the seals of the scroll (Rev 5:1–5), ultimately He alone is qualified to shepherd His people. Nevertheless, the ministries of the men God calls to be His shepherds must be consumed by His purpose for their lives. God's Word supplies clarity for this high calling.

The Shepherd God

In general, the Bible talks more about who a shepherd is than what a shepherd does. Yet, both are vital in ministry. They are combined in Asaph's tribute to David, "So he shepherded them according to the integrity of his heart, / And guided them by the skillfulness of his hands" (Ps 78:72).[1] This verse expresses the faithful integration of being and doing that completes the ideal shepherd.

Passages that are typically used to describe the role of the pastor (i.e., 1 Tim 3:1–7; Titus 1:5–9) address more of the character attributes required of pastors than they do actual functions. However, a few passages in Scripture speak to the tasks of pastoral ministry; among these are Jer 23:1–4; Ezek 34:1–10; Acts 20:17–36; Eph 4:11–12; and 1 Pet 5:1–4.

In Scripture the clearest picture of the functions of a shepherd is found in Ezekiel 34. In this chapter God outlines the responsibilities of shepherds, the accountability of the shepherds, the consequences of a lack of shepherds, and the anticipation of the good Shepherd. The responsibilities of a shepherd become clear as we examine those areas for which God holds His shepherd servants accountable. Thus, we understand what shepherds should do by paying attention to what God indicts them for not doing.

The potency of Ezekiel 34 is the clarity of God's instructions (i.e., what God expects of His servants)—not someone's idea of what God wants. God says what He demands—the "oughtness" of tending sheep. So, we should huddle in close and sit up straight at the anticipation of His instruction and, in sincere faith, say, "Speak, for your servant is listening."

What Shepherds Do

Being a pastor is hard work. The responsibilities seem endless. Some time ago, I put together a list of all the things that a pastor is expected to do. The list is still growing, but here is what I have so far. A pastor is expected to

---

[1] Other references to David as shepherd in Scripture are 1 Sam 16:11, 19; 17:15, 20, 34–36; 2 Sam 5:2; 1 Chr 17:6; 24:17; 21:17.

preach,
teach,
pray,
equip,
cast vision,
counsel,
lead the staff,
lead his family,
study,
conduct weddings and
funerals,

dedicate babies,
baptize,
serve the Lord's
Supper,
moderate business
meetings,
attend denominational
functions,
advise committees,
manage the public
relations of the
church,

lead the community in
social reform,
visit the sick and
the bereaved and
the lost and the
prospects and the
problematic,
provide leadership,
and
give direction.

But that is not all. In addition to what pastors are expected to do, there is also an unwritten list of expectations regarding what they should know. They are expected to be knowledgeable (maybe even an expert) in

theology,
hermeneutics,
rhetoric,
logic,
music,
architecture,
administration,
leadership,
management,
finance,
education,

conflict resolution,
worship,
counseling,
medicine,
legal matters,
ethics,
politics,
secular culture,
engineering,
acoustics,
aesthetics,

gerontology,
child-rearing,
apologetics,
evangelism,
etiquette,
prayer,
the Bible,
current events,
history,
religions, and
denominations.

To be fair, some of the expectations under which pastors operate are self-imposed; others are prescribed by the congregation. These tasks may be necessary or even good. But, they must not be the highest priorities. The church may employ you, but God is the One who called you. So, you must focus first on His instructions and filter all other expectations through the template of His Word.

Ezekiel 34 is God's message to pastors: "This is what I expect from you." He delivers these expectations in the context of His performance review of some shepherds who scored very low on their evaluations.

The indictment of the shepherds in Ezekiel 34 recalls God's search for a faithful leader in Ezek 22:30, "So I sought for a man among them who would make a wall and stand in the gap before Me on behalf of the land, that I should not destroy it; but I found no one."[2] It also highlights the fact that God will not leave His sheep unattended simply because His shepherds have not proven worthy of their calling.

Imagery of Shepherds and Sheep

Imagery of shepherd and sheep is common in Scripture and rich in significance.[3] The frequency of its use in the Pentateuch, in the history of the monarchy, in the book of Psalms, and in the Prophets demands careful exegetical attention.

The Bible uses shepherds and sheep as metaphors.[4] Metaphors do not define; they compare.[5] They explain what is unknown by comparing it to something that is known. Thus, when Jesus used metaphors to explain what "the kingdom of heaven is like," His intention was not to give us full comprehension of the kingdom. Instead, by comparison, we learn something about one aspect of His kingdom.

We must be careful not to press the image too far. There are obvious limitations to the images of sheep and shepherd. The portrayal of sheep as weak, sickly, and ignorant is not necessarily indicative of all church

---

[2] See Lamar Eugene Cooper, *Ezekiel*, NAC, vol. 17 (Nashville: B&H, 1994), 298. Cooper shows a relationship between Ezekiel 22 and 34, calling chapter 34 a "sequel" to chapter 22.

[3] See Andreas J. Köstenberger, "Jesus the Good Shepherd Who Will Also Bring Other Sheep (John 10:16): The Old Testament Background of a Familiar Metaphor," *BBR* 12, no. 1 (2002): 67–96 . Köstenberger suggests that the metaphors of sheep and shepherd are like an iceberg with much of their significance lying "under the surface" (75).

[4] Timothy S. Laniak, *Shepherds After My Own Heart: Pastoral Traditions and Leadership in the Bible*. (Downers Grove, IL: InterVarsity Press, 2006), 31–41. See also Köstenberger, "Jesus the Good Shepherd," 73–74, for a discussion on the distinction between metaphor and allegory.

[5] See Thomas Golding, "The Imagery of Shepherding in the Bible, Part 1," *BibSac* 163 (Jan–Mar, 2006): 19–21.

members. In addition, that sheep are often bred to be eaten might not sit well in a new members class.

Yet, the comforting assurance of a shepherd who leads his sheep to lush pastures and streams of refreshing water, protects them from impending dangers, cares for their needs, knows them individually, and seeks to find them when they are lost resonates in the church as much as in the pasture. That is the picture in Scripture of a God-honoring shepherd.

Who Were the Shepherds of Israel?

The term "shepherd" can mean a number of things in Scripture. It is used as both a noun and a verb. In addition to actual keepers of sheep, the term is used for kings and leaders in the Old Testament.[6] This is consistent with how the term was used in ancient Near Eastern literature.[7] In Ezekiel 34, given the context and the obvious connection with Jeremiah 23, the term clearly references the kings of Judah and other leaders entrusted with special care of God's people.[8] Moreover, the terms used to describe the intended functions of the shepherds convey the personal care expected of them by God.[9]

In the Old Testament, David is portrayed as the ultimate shepherd, even as Christ is portrayed as the true Shepherd in the New Testament. David served two shepherding functions in the Old Testament. He was an

---

[6] Cooper, *Ezekiel*, 298. See also Leslie C. Allen, *Ezekiel 20–48*, WBC, vol. 9 (Dallas: Word Books, 1990), 161; Iain Daguid, *Ezekiel*, NIVAC (Grand Rapids: Zondervan, 1999), 394; Walther Eichrodt, *Ezekiel: A Commentary* (Philadelphia: Westminster Press, 1970), 469; and Christopher J. H. Wright, *The Message of Ezekiel: A New Heart and a New Spirit*, The Bible Speaks Today (Leicester, UK; Downers Grove, IL: InterVarsity Press, 2001), 274. Cp. 2 Sam 5:2; 1 Kgs 22:17; Isa 44:28; Jer 2:8; 10:21; 23:1–4; 25:34–38; Mic 5:4–5; Zech 10:2–3; 11:3–17.

[7] Daniel Isaac Block, *The Book of Ezekiel Chapters 25–48*, NICOT (Grand Rapids: Eerdmans, 1997), 275. For a more extensive history of the use of the imagery outside of Scripture, see Jack W. Vancil, "Sheep, Shepherd," in *ABD*, ed. David Noel Freedman (New York: Doubleday, 1992), 5:1187–89; and Bernard Aubert, *The Shepherd-Flock Motif in the Miletus Discourse (Acts 20:17–38) Against Its Historical Background*, SBL 124 (New York: Peter Lang, 2009), 132–44.

[8] F. B. Huey, *Jeremiah, Lamentations*, NAC, vol. 16 (Nashville: B&H, 1993), 210. For more on the relationship between Ezekiel 34 and Jeremiah 23, see Block, 275–76.

[9] Jonathan David Huntzinger, "The End of Exile: A Short Commentary on the Shepherd/Sheep Metaphor in Exilic and Post-Exilic Prophetic and Synoptic Gospel Literature," PhD diss., Fuller Theological Seminary, 1999, 150–51.

actual shepherd (1 Sam 16:11); and, as king, he was the shepherd-leader of his people (Ps 78:70–72). Thus, as David's early role as a shepherd of his father's sheep foreshadowed his later role as shepherd of Israel, so his life became a type of the true Shepherd of God's people ultimately fulfilled in Christ.[10]

God as Shepherd

The imagery of a shepherd is not limited to mankind. In Scripture, God is both called[11] and portrayed as a shepherd.[12] Moreover, the Bible frequently refers to God's people as His sheep.[13] So, if God is the true Shepherd, then the role of His under-shepherd must find its meaning in Him. Thus, the essential question of Ezekiel 34 is: What does it mean to be a shepherd?

Jesus as the Good Shepherd

The conscious expectation of the Shepherd-Messiah in the Old Testament finds its fulfillment in Christ.[14] He is also described as "the good shepherd" (John 10:11, 14); the "one shepherd" (John 10:16), the "great Shepherd" (Heb 13:20), and "the Chief Shepherd" (1 Pet 5:4).[15] In the New Testament, Jesus completes the Messianic promise of Ezekiel

---

[10] See Köstenberger, "Jesus the Good Shepherd," 77.

[11] Gen 49:24; Pss 23:1; 80:1; Heb 13:20. Cp. Isa 30:23; 40:11; Mic 7:14. See also Quentin P. Kinnison, "Shepherd or One of the Sheep: Revisiting the Biblical Metaphor of the Pastorate," *JRL* 9, no. 1 (2010): 71. Kinnison helpfully points out that in Scripture, God is only ever identified as Shepherd of a singular flock, not of plural flocks.

[12] Gen 48:15; 49:23–24; 2 Sam 5:2; Pss 23:1–3; 28:9; 77:20; 78:52; 79:13; 80:1; 95:7; 100:3; 119:176; Ecc 12:11; Isa 40:11; 53:6; 63:11; Jer 3:15; 23:1–4; 31:10; 50:7; Hos 4:16; Mic 2:12; 5:4; 7:14; Zech 10:2–3; 11:16; Matt 2:6; 18:12–14; 25:32–46; Luke 12:32; 15:3–7; John 10:11, 14; 11:52; 21:15–19; Acts 20:28–29; Heb 13:20; 1 Pet 2:25; 5:2–4; Rev 7:17.

[13] Pss 95:7; 100:3; Isa 40:11; 53:6; Jer 31:10; Zech 9:6; 13:7; Matt 10:6, 16; John 10:3, 9, 11, 14, 27; Acts 20:28; 1 Pet 2:25.

[14] Matt 9:6; 15:24; 25:32–33; 26:31–35; John 10:1–18, 25–28; Heb 13:20–21; 1 Pet 2:25; 5:4; Rev 7:15–17.

[15] The good Shepherd has compassion for His sheep (Matt 9:36) and knows His sheep by name (John 10:3, 14, 27); the sheep know His voice (John 10:3–5, 14, 16, 27), and He sacrificially lays down His life for His sheep (John 10:11, 15, 17–18).

34.[16] Jesus stands in antithetical relationship to the false shepherds (John 10:1, 5, 8, 10, 12–13):

- He knows the sheep, and the sheep know Him (John 10:3, 14, 27).
- He leads the sheep (John 10:4).
- He protects the sheep (John 10:10).
- He is a good shepherd (John 10:11, 14).
- He sacrifices Himself for the sheep (John 10:11, 15).
- He feeds the sheep (Isa 40:11; John 21:15–17).
- He holds the shepherds accountable (1 Pet 5:4).
- He is "the Chief Shepherd" (Heb 13:20).

Ironically, He is both Lamb and Shepherd.[17]

Pastors as Shepherds

The New Testament applies the image of the shepherd to the role of pastor. In contrast to the faithless shepherds of the Old Testament, shepherds in the New Testament are never pictured as unfaithful.[18] Although the term "shepherd" is applied to pastors only once in the New Testament (Eph 4:11), the functions of a shepherd are frequently apparent in descriptions of their responsibilities. Pastors should care for the congregation (Acts 20:28; 1 Pet 5:2–4), seek the lost (Matt 18:12–14), protect the flock (Acts 20:29), feed the flock (John 21:15–17),[19] and oversee the flock (1 Pet 5:2). Moreover, the word "shepherd" occurs in verbal form to describe the work of a pastor (Matt 2:6; John 21:16; Acts 20:28; 1 Pet 5:2) even as the word "sheep" is used to describe God's people (John 10:14–16, 26–27).

One can preach *to* the sheep, but one can only pastor *among* the sheep. Being a pastor requires proximity to the sheep. "Preacher" is a title earned

---

[16] For a discussion on Jesus as the supreme model and fulfillment of Ezekiel 34, see Daguid, *Ezekiel*, 400–1.

[17] Kinnison, "Shepherd or One of the Sheep," 83. See also Charles Edward Jefferson, *The Minister as Shepherd* (New York: Thomas & Crowell company, 1912), 31; https://archive.org/details/ministerasshephe00jeff.

[18] Joiachim Jeremias, "ποιμήν [...]," in *TDNT*, ed. Gerhard Kittel and Gerhard Friedrich, trans. Geoffrey W. Bromiley (Grand Rapids: Eerdmans, 1968), 6:490.

[19] Ibid., 498.

by excellence in education and eloquence, but "Pastor" is a title earned by hands-on ministry. Correspondingly, Jefferson notes that the affection of church members for their pastor is more intimate than their affection for leaders serving in other ministry positions. Eloquent preachers may be admired, but faithful pastors are loved.[20] Serving as pastor involves more intimate connection with the sheep. Nathan's fictional allegory of a man with one little lamb describes the affection of a true shepherd for the individual members of his flock (2 Sam 12:1–4). Such is the calling of a biblical shepherd.

A Message of Woe

Ezekiel 34 begins with a charge from the Lord to the prophet to "prophesy against" the shepherds of Israel. In verses 2–3, the text's perspective changes from third person to second person as the message shifts from God's instructions for Ezekiel to Ezekiel's message for the shepherds.

However, the origin of the message is not in question. It is God's indictment of His shepherds. Five times the expression "Thus says the Lord God" (vv. 2, 10–11, 17, 20) is found; four times, the phrase "says the Lord God" (vv. 8, 15, 30–31); and twice, the admonition to "hear the word of the Lord" (vv. 7, 9). Ezekiel is simply delivering God's message, and His shepherds are expected to pay attention.

I find it curious that God does not speak *to* the shepherds. Perhaps these were not shepherds at all. Instead, the picture reveals that they were more akin to Jesus's description of "the hireling" (John 10:12–13), whose concern for his own safety overshadowed the needs of the sheep. Thus, the contrast between the shepherding work of God in Ezek 34:11–16 and the failure of the anti-shepherds in 34:1–10 parallels that of the good Shepherd, who is the antithesis of "the hireling" (John 10:11).

The shepherds of Israel were not the first group against whom the Lord directed Ezekiel to prophesy. Of the 17 times the Lord instructed His prophets to "prophesy against" someone, 15 of those were entrusted to Ezekiel. Ezekiel was instructed to prophesy against Jerusalem (4:7), the

---

[20] Jefferson, *The Minister as Shepherd*, 109–10.

mountains of Israel (6:2), the wicked counselors in Israel (11:4), the false prophets of Israel (13:2), the false female prophets (13:17), the forest in the south of Israel (20:46), the land of Israel (21:2), the Ammonites (25:2), Sidon (28:21), "Pharaoh king of Egypt" (29:2), the shepherds of Israel (34:2), Mount Seir (35:2), and Gog (38:2; 39:1). Ezekiel functions as the prophet "against."

The force of this message is that it was not addressed to other nations or even to the sinful people of Israel, but to their intended spiritual leaders. In a declaration of woe first uttered by Jeremiah (Jer 23:1) and later echoed by Zechariah (Zech 11:17), God through Ezekiel pronounced a message of woe against the shepherds.[21]

Counterfeit Shepherds

Football fans will remember the 2012 National Football League Referees Association labor dispute, which resulted in a referee lockout. Throughout the preseason and the first part of the regular season, regular referees were replaced by less skilled substitutes. As the drama of these referees began to unfold, stories emerged about the background of the men assuming those roles. Some came to the NFL from six-man football, some had been fired from previous referee positions for incompetence, and at least one had been fired from his previous referee job with the Lingerie Football League.

The outcome of this experiment led to more than just blown calls and the slowing down of the games. It resulted in a lack of respect for the role of the official, situations where the refs appeared to have been intimidated by coaches and players with strong personalities, outrage in the media, and general disgust and distrust from the fans.

Despite all the apologizing, overanalyzing, and fining of players and coaches, I do not know anyone who believed that these men intended to do a poor job. However, what became clear is that they were immersed in

---

[21] On the relationship of Ezekiel 34 to Jeremiah 23, see Block, *The Book of Ezekiel: Chapters 25–48*, 276; and Allen, *Ezekiel 20–48*, 161. See also, Walther Zimmerli, *Ezekiel 1: A Commentary on the Book of Ezekiel, Chapters 1–24*, trans. R. E. Clements, Hermeneia (Philadelphia: Fortress, 1979), 245. Huntzinger regards Ezekiel 34 as a development of Jeremiah 23 ("The End of Exile," 111, 152–53).

a challenge over their heads. It was as if they were unprepared for the job. Each substitute was wearing someone else's jersey.

With all the questions related to inconsistencies, the missed calls, delays in the game, and the breakdowns in communication, I began to see a parallel to the role of a pastor today. We live in a time when every decision pastors make is analyzed, scrutinized, and criticized. Some churches have even initiated a sort of "review process" for the decisions of the pastor that do much more than simply slow down the pace of the game. Further, I have also witnessed pastors intimidated by strong personalities in the church, and others all too often have been fired from their positions. The result has been that pastors no longer enjoy the level of respect formerly common to that position.

To be fair, some of the problems evidenced by the replacement referees have at times been reflected in pastors. Failures in communication, missed "calls," and underqualified leaders have yielded the self-inflicted wounds that sting so many churches today. Then, as the media continues to accentuate these evident failures, church members—like disenchanted fans—eventually lose confidence in the position and sometimes even in the game itself. And, like the NFL stadiums, churches feel the effects in declines in attendance and giving.

But, there is one key difference between a backup referee and a pastor. Unlike the replacement officials, who were on the field against the wishes of the "real" refs, undershepherds serve in the authority, power, and calling of the true Shepherd. Just as "sheep are not independent travelers,"[22] so shepherds are not independent contractors. They report to the Chief Shepherd.

The shepherds under indictment in Ezekiel 34 were more than just mistaken; they were not just shepherds who had fallen out of line. They were counterfeits, anti-shepherds,[23] "predatory misrulers."[24] As such, God castigated them for their callous self-indulgence, exploiting the sheep for their own benefit (v. 2); for their failure to meet the needs of the flock

---

[22] Jefferson, *The Minister as Shepherd*, 40.
[23] Huntzinger, "The End of Exile," 96.
[24] Moshe Greenberg, *Ezekiel 21–37: A New Translation with Introduction and Commentary*, AB (New York: Doubleday, 1997): 708.

(v. 3); for their lack of concern for the flock (v. 4); and for their ruling the flock with force and cruelty (v. 4).

These anti-shepherds personally gained—they "feed themselves" (vv. 2, 10)—from ministry but failed in its obligations.[25] They expected the best from the sheep but gave little in return. They ravaged the sheep[26] despite the inherent counter-productivity of doing so.[27]

Consequences of the Shepherds' Irresponsibility

The consequences brought on by these counterfeit shepherds were catastrophic.[28] God revealed that His sheep had become weak, sick, and broken (v. 4); they had been driven away (v. 4), lost (v. 4) and scattered from the flock (vv. 4–6);[29] they had wandered in search of care (v. 6); they had become prey among the nations (vv. 8, 28); they had been devoured by wild beasts (vv. 5, 28); and they suffered from fear (v. 28), hunger (v. 29), and shame (v. 29).[30]

The phrase "like sheep having no shepherd" (Matt 9:36)[31] capsulizes the paradigmatic equation describing the aftermath of a shepherd's absence. These anti-shepherds were occupying a position, but they were not really shepherds. And the sheep paid the price.

Because of their failure to shepherd the sheep, these false shepherds were called to account before the Lord (vv. 5–10).[32] Twice, God called on them to "hear" (vv. 7, 9). He delineated the charges in verses 4 and 5 and

---

[25] See Jefferson, *The Minister as Shepherd*, 35–6. Jefferson asserts that a shepherd's task "is a humble work; such is has been from the beginning and such it must be to the end. A man must come down to do it. A shepherd doesn't shine. He cannot cut a figure. His work must be done in obscurity."

[26] Cp. Ezek 34:3.

[27] Clearly if one is not properly caring for the sheep, ultimately one will have less to consume later.

[28] For other indictments against shepherds, see Isa 56:9–12; Jer 10:21; 23:1–4; 50:6–7; Zech 10:2–3; 11:4–17.

[29] For a good discussion of the Hebrew words used to describe the condition of the sheep, see Huntzinger, "The End of Exile," 97, 100, 113–16.

[30] To that list could also be added the "the lean sheep" (v. 20).

[31] Cp. Num 27:16–7; 1 Kgs 22:17; 2 Chr 18:16; Ezek 34:5; Nah 3:18; Zech 10:2; 13:7; Mark 6:34; 14:27.

[32] See Jer 23:2 for a play on words in Hebrew. God told the shepherds that because they did not attend to the sheep, God would attend to them.

then reiterated them in verse 8. The force of His arraignment is felt in the words, "I am against the shepherds" (v. 10).

The consequences for these scatterers of God's flock were both immediate and ultimate. They "must give account."[33] God said, "I will require My flock at their hand; I will cause them to cease feeding the sheep, and the shepherds shall feed themselves no more; for I will deliver My flock from their mouths that they may no longer be food for them" (v. 10).[34] Therefore, God declared that He was going to take away from the shepherds their flock, their position, and their benefits. Their removal was both judgment for the shepherds and grace for the sheep. Shepherds must remember that ministry is a privilege, not a right. Those who are found to be unworthy forfeit the privilege accessible only by His grace.

Scripture reveals that there are two categories of accusations against the shepherds. The fourfold repetition of the word "scattered" in verses 4–6 accentuates the outcome for the sheep in both cases.

The first accusation against the shepherds regards what they did not do. Verses 3 and 4 reveal how the shepherds neglected the sheep.[35] Worse, the shepherds' omission is juxtaposed with what they did for themselves. They ate the best sheep and clothed themselves with wool from the flocks (v. 2).[36] Thus, the sheep were scattered because of the inaction of the shepherds (vv. 4, 6).

The second accusation against the shepherds pertained to what they did. The scattering described in verse 5 was the direct result of their actions. They ruled their sheep with force and cruelty. Here, the savagery of the shepherds caused the scattering of the sheep.

---

[33] Heb 13:17; cp. Luke 16:2; Rom 14:12; 1 Pet 3:15; 4:5.

[34] See Young S. Chae, *Jesus as the Eschatological Davidic Shepherd: Studies in the Old Testament, Second Temple Judaism, and in the Gospel of Matthew*, WUNT 2, 216 (Tübingen: Mohr Siebeck, 2006), 59–60. Chae notes that in 34:10, God places the false shepherds into the category of "wild beasts" and describes the process of delivering the sheep from their mouths.

[35] See Laniak, *Shepherds After My Own* Heart, 152. Laniak explains that negligence was "tantamount to abuse."

[36] The ironies in the passage are thick: The shepherds fed and clothed themselves, but did not feed and clothe the sheep. Because the shepherds did not feed the sheep, the sheep became food for beasts.

The shepherds' failure to care for their sheep proved that they were not true shepherds at all. What these derelict shepherds *were* doing demonstrated that actually they were false shepherds. Some sheep were scattered because of the absence of a true shepherd (i.e., what the shepherds did not do). Others were scattered because of the presence of a false shepherd (i.e., what the shepherds did do). The accusations accentuate the contrast in verses 11–16, in which God delineated what *He* would do for the sheep in the absence of the shepherds. He would do what they had failed to do, and He would undo what they had done.

My Sheep

Sometimes ministers are careless in their use of pronouns. The pronoun "my" implies possession. Pastors often say "my church" or "my people" when referring to the the congregation or "flock" they serve. Usually, the implications are harmless, and most people know what they mean. However, one might be wise to remind himself that the sheep do not belong to the earthly shepherd.

God is very particular in His use of pronouns in Ezekiel 34. He makes the distinction clear, referring to His people 15 times as "My flock" (vv. 6, 8, 10, 15, 17, 19, 22, 31) or "My sheep"[37] (vv. 6, 11–12) and once as "My people" (v. 30). He also talks about "My shepherds" (v. 8), "My servant David" (vv. 23–24), "My hills" (v. 26), and "My pasture" (v. 31). You hear echoes of this in the Lord's challenge to Peter in John 21, where the restored disciple is three times challenged to feed "My lambs" and "My sheep."[38]

Clearly, then, the shepherds have no claim of possession, and their authority over the sheep is only imputed. As shepherds, we need to remind ourselves regularly that God's sheep do not belong to us. We simply have the task to care for them until the true Shepherd returns.

---

[37] See Wright, *The Message of Ezekiel*, 275. Wright explains that the same Hebrew word (*tso'n*) is translated as "flock" and "sheep" in Ezekiel 34.

[38] See also John 10:14–27 and 21:15–17 for Jesus's use of "My sheep" and "My lambs."

Outline of Ezekiel 34

The framework of Ezekiel 34 is masterful. The chapter contains two almost equal halves, which are each divided into two parts. The organization is obvious. Part 1 stands in parallel with part 3, and part 2 parallels part 4.[39]

  I. The False Shepherds (vv. 1–10)
   A. Indictment of the Shepherds (vv. 1–2)
   B. Responsibility of the Shepherds (vv. 3–4)
   C. Consequences of Their Irresponsibility (vv. 5–6)
   D. Accountability of the Shepherds (vv. 7–10)
 II. The True Shepherd (vv. 11–16)
III. Accountability of the Sheep (vv. 17–22)
   A. Indictment of the Sheep (v. 17)
   B. Responsibility of the Sheep (vv. 18–19)
   C. Consequences of Their Irresponsibility (v. 20)
   D. Accountability of the Sheep (v. 21)
IV. Divine Provision for the Sheep (vv. 23–31)
   A. The One Shepherd (vv. 23–24)
   B. A Covenant of Peace (vv. 25–29)
   C. Divine Affirmation (vv. 30–31)

The Functions of a Shepherd

The primary intention of this book is to examine the areas for which God holds His shepherds accountable and to understand the expectations He has for His leaders today. As we examine God's contentions against the false shepherds of Israel, His expectations become clear. We are accountable before God in these same areas. Fundamentally, shepherds are responsible for caring for the needs of the sheep.[40] How ministers carry

---

[39] Parts 1 and 3 are exact parallels. Parts 2 and 4 are parallel with the description of what the true Shepherd will do. However, Part 4 concludes with the covenant promise and the divine affirmation to the sheep.

[40] Thomas A. Golding, "The Imagery of Shepherding in the Bible, Part 2." *BibSac* 163 (Apr–June 2006): 173.

out these functions may vary with each context, but the functions remain the same.

Shepherds Must Feed the Flock (vv. 2–3, 8, 10, 19)

The phrase "First things first" expresses the idea that whatever is most essential should be addressed before anything else. As the Lord unveiled His most extended message on the responsibilities of a shepherd, His attention focused first on the nourishment of His sheep. Shepherds feed their sheep. This responsibility is outlined five times in Ezekiel 34 (vv. 2–3, 8, 10, 19). Another four times, the Lord promised His personal involvement in the feeding process (vv. 13–15, 23).

That someone would make his living by being a shepherd but fail to feed the sheep seems unconscionable. Yet that is exactly the accusation the Lord made regarding the overweight and stingy shepherds of Judah (34:2).

To become so enamored with the meat of God's Word that we find ourselves skimpy with the sheep is an enticing temptation. Maybe it is the unearthing of a *hapax legomenon* or the rich nuances of a lemma that sequesters us in our study. Perhaps it is the diversion of the newest study resource that arrests our attention and subjugates our time. These are good things, to be sure; but when they become the focus and not the lens, they become excuses for avoiding the sheep rather than resources to nourish them.

Consider the pre-flight instructions given to parents regarding oxygen masks for their children. They are told that in the event of an emergency, oxygen masks will drop from the ceiling. Then, almost counterintuitively, parents are instructed to put on their own masks first, and *then* take care of their children. Just as oxygen-deprived parents cannot effectively administer oxygen to their children, so underfed shepherds cannot feed sheep. But, shepherds must never allow the sheep to starve while they alone enjoy the green of the pasture. They must remember that spiritual food is not only for the shepherd.

The subtle and significant danger is this: because we deal with excellent words, thoughts, and ideas, we easily gorge ourselves with the meaty truths of God's Word (like Eli at the dinner table) and leave the sheep to scavenge only on our leftovers. The obviousness of the obvious strikes us:

The Lord expects the shepherds to feed the sheep. David Allen will talk more about this in chapter 2.

Shepherds Must Strengthen the Weak (v. 4)

Scripture reveals the heart of the heavenly Father for the vulnerable. He commands special care for those who are poor, sick, widowed, or distressed. Indeed, James suggested that the definition of pure and undefiled religion begins with visiting orphans and widows in their distress (Jas 1:27). God's concern for the weak is also seen in Scripture. Failing to strengthen the weak is the second dereliction of the shepherds in Ezekiel 34.

Immediately after the discussion of feeding the sheep, the Lord's attention turned to strengthening the weak. Sadly, shepherds too often spend an inordinate amount of time caressing the strong sheep rather than strengthening the weak ones. But the Bible reminds us that sheep are prone to weaknesses.

Consider an example from sports. Teams named for animals are typically named for strong ones. For example, we have tigers, bears, rams, chargers, colts, and panthers. You do not see sheep in that list. Sheep are not intimidating. They tend to be defenseless, slow, unintelligent, and subject to disease.

Because of the weakness of the sheep, the Lord castigates the shepherds for not strengthening them (34:4). Shepherds are responsible for being ever alert to the signs indicating that a sheep is in trouble. Anything less becomes little more than dignified hypocrisy. We cannot be so preoccupied with matters of our own choosing, while the shepherd-deprived sheep languish enfeebled and "un-strengthened."

When a sheep is weak is probably not the time to lecture that sheep on the dangers of careless living any more than a home fire is the time to research the history of firefighting. Instead, shepherds must look for ways to remove the weaknesses of the sheep. Perhaps then they are better able to understand the ultimate provision of the One who "gives power to the weak, / And to those who have no might He increases strength" (Isa 40:29). I will talk more about this in chapter 3.

Shepherds Must Heal the Sick (v. 4)

When Jesus sent out the Twelve, He appointed them to both preach and heal (Luke 9:2).[41] Later, He reminded the sanctimonious Pharisees that those who are whole do not need a physician, "but those who are sick" (Luke 5:31). Finally, as He admonished the goats on His left, He explained, "I was sick . . . and you did not visit Me" (Matt 25:43).

Indeed, if people who are sick cannot turn to the church, where can they turn? I have often said that in church work, you never know how much you need the church until you need the church. The servant of the Lord must be both preacher and physician. In ministry, we encounter people with wounds medical doctors cannot see and with sicknesses that health insurance cannot cover.

Few things are worse to see than something or someone not carrying out the function for which they exist. Like clouds that never rain, ministers who cannot heal perpetuate the unfulfilled anticipation of those who have sought but have not found.

To be sure, not all who are sick suffer from the same maladies, nor will one treatment be universally effective. Some may be sick physically, others spiritually. Some will suffer diseases of conviction, others of a wounded heart. Some will be infirm from bereavement; others, from estrangement. Thus, the shepherd must be widely familiar with the science of spiritual therapeutics, understanding that the Lord grants grace at the bedside as well as in the pulpit.

Healing may come through your comfort, counsel, and care, or perhaps merely through your presence. The type of care required depends on the nature of the condition. In order to understand the sicknesses of the sheep and apply the appropriate care, as a faithful shepherd, you must be "diligent to know the state of your flocks" (Prov 27:23).[42]

As believers, we know that the only true healing is through the act of God in Christ and is only fully realized upon His return. Yet God expects that His servants will be agents of healing, availing themselves of the spiritual

---

[41] Jefferson, *The Minister as Shepherd*, 38.

[42] For a helpful discussion on the importance of knowing the condition of the flock, see Kevin Leman and William Pentak, *The Way of the Shepherd: 7 Ancient Secrets to Managing Productive People* (Grand Rapids: Zondervan, 2004), 15–28.

power He extends to them to render aid for whatever ailments may be encountered. Paige Patterson will talk more about this in chapter 4.

Shepherds Must Bind Up the Broken (v. 4)

My wife and I have four boys. One of the things you learn quickly with multiple males in the household is that the world is a dangerous place. Boys aren't looking for beauty; they are looking for adventure. But with great adventure comes great risk.

In our case, when our boys were young, injuries were a somewhat common occurrence. Among other things, we experienced six broken arms. I remember one spring when our twin boys wore casts simultaneously, casualties of the same playground only two days apart (and we got a call each time from the same school nurse). I vividly remember, in every case, the helplessness of a non-medically trained father sitting in the ER with a child hurting from a broken arm I could not fix. My earnest wish to trade places with my son was drowned out only by my fervent prayers to the true Healer.

Broken bones usually heal, but in ministry we deal with hurts of a much more lasting nature. Some of the wounds we encounter are physical, some are spiritual, and some are emotional. Only the timely salve of truth from God's Word, the love of the heavenly Father, and the hope of eternal life delivered through a caring shepherd can heal hurts X-ray machines will never reveal.

The Lord holds shepherds responsible for binding up the broken among the sheep. In context, this charge occurs immediately after acknowledgment of the shepherd's failure to heal the sick. However, binding that which is broken demands an even more personal connection than healing.

The Lord turned to this aspect in His message in the synagogue:

The Spirit of the Lord God is upon Me,
Because He has anointed Me
To preach the gospel to the poor;
He has sent Me to heal the brokenhearted,
To proclaim liberty to captives

And recovery of sight to the blind,
To set at liberty those who are oppressed;
To proclaim the acceptable year of the Lord. (Luke 4:16–19)

One thing is certain: We will not bind up the broken from a distance; we will not bring healing to people's lives by dictate, rebuke, persuasion, or even good intentions. Healing requires touch. It requires proximity. It is hands-on, close contact. The kinds of hurts most people encounter won't be assuaged by an email, a tweet, or a post on social media. Shepherds touch sheep. They hold them.[43]

One of the few things I know with certainty about pastoral ministry is that if you do not like people, you are not going to be a good shepherd. Indeed, one of the primary reasons why pastoral tenures are so shockingly brief today is because too many shepherds never get close to their sheep. You cannot do the work of a pastor from a distance. A preacher may sequester himself in his study, but the work of a pastor begins in the hearts of the people he touches.

Shepherds who fail to bind that which is broken have embezzled God's authority and wasted its privilege. If even the world knows that the first responsibility of a physician is to do no harm, shouldn't shepherds of our Lord follow that dictum and more? The sorrow of our Lord's rebuke revealed the irony of caregivers who administered no care. Like the religious leader who passed by the injured man on the other side of the road is the pastor who does not bind up the broken among his sheep. Dale Johnson will talk more about this in chapter 5.

Shepherds Must Protect the Flock (vv. 5, 8)

Years ago, in the once-popular police television drama *Hill Street Blues,* every episode climaxed with Sergeant Esterhaus completing roll call with the admonition to his officers, "Let's be careful out there." This phrase circulated as that generation's version of "going viral" because it captured the stark reality of which we are all too often reminded today:

---

[43] See Jefferson, *The Minister as Shepherd*, 126: "Physicians never deal with men in crowds. . . . [they deal with them] 'one patient at a time.'"

police work is dangerous business. In a very similar way, pastors must be so reminded of the dangers of their work, and they must assiduously protect the sheep.

Twice in Ezekiel 34 (vv. 5, 8) the Lord rebuked the shepherds for their failure to protect the sheep. The sheep were scattered and ran away when danger approached and were overpowered by an enemy who was more powerful "because there was no shepherd." The shepherds had become selfishly concerned about their own needs and ignored those of the vulnerable sheep.

The fact that the Lord has chosen the image of sheep to describe His people is both appropriate and relevant, despite an increasingly urban society. Sheep are vulnerable. They do not possess the ability to defend themselves from predators, and they are too slow to outrun them. Moreover, it is not always clear that they are smart enough to identify impending danger. Thus, failure on the part of the shepherd to protect them is tantamount to ministerial treason.

Upon Paul's completion of a three-year ministry in Ephesus, he challenged the church leaders in Acts 20 to "take heed to yourselves and to the flock." To do that they were instructed to watch and warn the sheep over whom they had been made overseers. Paul cautioned the leaders that after his departure, "savage wolves" would come to attack the sheep, implying both the reality of dangers to the sheep and the fact that Paul had protected them.

Shepherds must watch and warn. They cannot just ignore the wolves that move ever closer to the sheep. The shepherd must stand in the gap, declaring to the wolves of the world that they can only get to the sheep through him. He must be vigilant in guarding the door and watching the exits for possible dangers ahead. When false truth and weak theology threaten the fellowship, the shepherd must warn the sheep. When the church blurs the lines of right and wrong, the shepherd must disambiguate the message. When technology makes compromise convenient, the shepherd must courageously expose it. And when absolute truth is mocked, the shepherd must lovingly, passionately, persuasively, and relentlessly defend it as the foundation of our faith and the bedrock of our authority. Wrong is not wrong because the world disagrees with it; it is wrong because God declared it to be so. Where there is no absolute right, there can be no consensus on what is wrong.

Faithful shepherds cannot be found sleeping while the sheep are in peril. They cannot flee when danger approaches. They must watch over the flock, and they must warn the sheep. The world can be a dangerous place, especially if you are a sheep. Malcolm Yarnell will talk more about this in chapter 6.

Shepherds Must Bring Back Those Driven Away (vv. 4, 6, 8)

Just as the 5,000 hungry congregants were about to leave to secure food for themselves, Jesus directed the disciples, "They do not need to go away. [They need you to] give them something to eat" (Matt 14:16).

In our fixation on the last part of Jesus's instructions, we have missed the emphasis on the former. While the sheep need to be fed, they do not need to go away. The idea is that this is where they need to be. Yet, like wandering sheep, too often, crowds are going away from the church today. The Lord reminds in Scripture that these sheep, too, are the responsibility of the shepherd. The church today has become all too comfortable with the "back door," allowing the exit of as many sheep as the "front door" welcomes.

The Lord rebuked the unfaithful shepherds in Ezekiel 34 for their lack of concern for the sheep who had wandered away.[44] The sheep had wandered and become prey (v. 5; cp. John 10:12); they had been scattered across the world (Ezek 34:5–6; cp. 1 Kgs 22:7) and, most significantly, no one was going after them (Ezek 34:6, 8; cp. Jer 10:21). Sadly, the shepherds were both unfaithful and unconcerned.

To be sure, sheep wander for a variety of reasons—some for their own sin, some due to the oppression of the enemy, and some because of the shepherd's carelessness. Regardless of why they are missing, the shepherd's job is to cause them to return.

---

[44] See Timothy Z. Witmer, *The Shepherd Leader: Achieving Effective Shepherding in Your Church.* (Phillipsburg, NJ: P&R, 2010), 83: "In so many cases church leaders do not even perceive that their people have strayed. What does it mean to stray if there are no fences?"

Shepherds are not given the luxury of customizing the sheep in their congregations. Nor are we allowed the alternative of dismissing some wandering sheep because we like the fact that they are no longer in the fold or because we perceive that retrieving them is not worth the effort.

When the sheep are scattered, regardless of why they are gone, the shepherd's mandate is to bring them back. Shepherds cannot simply focus on bringing in new sheep and disregard bringing back those who have left. They must follow the example of the good Shepherd and be moved again with compassion for all the sheep. Tommy Kiker will talk more about this in chapter 7.

Shepherds Must Seek the Lost (vv. 4, 6, 8, 11–12, 16)

The 1982 movie *Star Trek II: The Wrath of Khan* was famous for the phrase, "The needs of the many outweigh the needs of the few." In the movie, Spock sacrificed his life to save the ship and all those on her by exposing himself to a lethal dosage of radiation to repair the damaged engineering deck. However, in the sequel, *Star Trek III: The Search for Spock,* Admiral Kirk and the crew risk their lives, their careers, and even the Federation to rescue Spock, who had been regenerated but had no memory of his career on the starship *Enterprise*. At the climax of the movie, Spock realized the lengths to which Kirk went to rescue him, and he asked the admiral why he would go to such effort to save a friend. Kirk replied, "Because the needs of the one outweigh the needs of the many."[45]

Although just a movie, and perhaps not logical, the message is true. Sometimes the needs of the one do outweigh the needs of the many. Scripture affirms this principle. Jesus told the story of a shepherd who was willing to leave the 99 sheep (possibly risking their safety in his absence) to search for one sheep that was lost. In that moment, the urgency for the salvation of the lost outweighed the necessity to preserve the security of the found!

---

[45] *Star Trek II: The Wrath of Khan* (1982; Los Angeles: Paramount Studios), directed by Nicholas Meyer; *Star Trek III: The Search for Spock* (1984; Los Angeles: Paramount Studios), directed by Leonard Nimoy.

Only in understanding the heart of a shepherd who would leave the 99 "unlost" sheep to seek the one that is "unfound" does one begin to understand the heart of a true shepherd. The unmistakable charge of every shepherd is to search after lost sheep. In the work of shepherds, one must not immerse all our ministry resources in managing "found" people. True shepherds also seek the lost.

Shepherds must seek the sheep because they are perishing (v. 4), scattered (v. 5), prey for beasts (v. 5), and wandering (v. 6). Shepherds must seek lost sheep out of genuine love for them and obedience to the command of the true Shepherd. The last thing the text mentions that the evil shepherds did *not* do (v. 8) is the first thing mentioned that the good Shepherd does (v. 11). Shepherds must be willing to leave the safety of the pen and go rescue sheep from the dangers inherent in lostness. Matt Queen will talk more about this in chapter 8.

Shepherds Must Lead the Flock (vv. 6, 13–14, 21)

Sometimes we are better at talking about things than actually doing them. Nowhere is this more evident than in the topic of leadership. Pass through any bookstore and you will find shelves of books on leadership, leadership principles, leadership keys, and leadership secrets according to [fill in the blank]. Oddly, most would agree that despite the prevalence of leadership resources, leadership ability has not improved noticeably.

But the problem is not unique to our time. The need for shepherd-leaders completes the list of accusations the Lord made against the shepherds in Ezekiel 34. The Lord's grief was evident as He announced that His sheep wandered from the fold and dwelt in insecurity because their shepherds were not leading them. The absence of shepherd leadership resulted in wandering, unsafe, confused, and hungry sheep. The Lord identified the problem in verse 21, noting that the shepherds' attempts at leadership consisted of trying to push the sheep around rather than leading them. But, one does not lead from behind. You do not drive sheep; you lead them. You do not shoo them; you woo them. Sheep lie down in green pastures because the shepherd has made them feel safe.

The answer might not be found in a book, but it will be evident in the field. Good shepherds do not lead by proxy, dictate demands, or achieve goals by good intentions. Shepherds live among the sheep and carefully and consistently lead the sheep from where they are to where they should be. Fred Luter will talk more about this in chapter 9.

The True Shepherd

Ezekiel 34 does not just tell us what shepherds should do; it tells us what the true Shepherd will do.[46] The highlight of this chapter is the reminder that God has not simply outsourced shepherding. He will personally care for His sheep.

Ultimately, the failure of God's shepherds did not go unnoticed. He held His shepherds accountable, but that did not mitigate the damage they caused. The shepherdless sheep needed to be tended. So, God Himself assumed that responsibility. He did not leave His sheep unattended. David conveyed the comfort of a contented sheep when he recounted in Psalm 23 that with the Lord as his shepherd, he would not want (23:1) and he would not fear (23:4).[47] Such is the comfort of sheep under the care of the true Shepherd.

The juxtaposition between the false shepherds and the true Shepherd is seen most clearly in a comparison of verses 4 and 16. Verse 4 delineates what the shepherds of Israel did not do, while verse 16 affirms what God will do. Thus, as Daguid asserts, "[T]he change to be wrought in Israel's situation is not so much a change in the nature of the office as in the nature of the occupant."[48]

The assurance of God's promise to His sheep is seen in the 21 occurrences of the phrase, "I will."[49] Like a 21-gun salute, God declares His sovereignty over the shepherds and compassion for the sheep. His "I will" becomes the ultimate solution for the "did nots" of the anti-shepherds.

---

[46] For the juxtaposition of judgment and promise in Ezekiel 34, see Daguid, *Ezekiel*, 394; and Huntzinger, "The End of Exile," 109. See also Allen, who explains how the claims suggesting that repetition within the chapter equals redaction are unwarranted (*Ezekiel 20–48*, 159).

[47] Cp. Ps 23:2 and Ezek 34:15, "I will make them lie down."

[48] Daguid, *Ezekiel*, 396.

[49] For a discussion of the promises of God in this section, see Cooper, *Ezekiel*, 301.

Twelve different verbs in rapid succession emphatically attest to what God will do for the sheep. He will "search" for (v. 11), "seek" out (v. 11), "deliver" (v. 12), "bring" out (v. 13), "gather" (v. 13), "bring" to (v. 13), "feed" (vv. 13–15), "make . . . [to] lie down" (v. 15), "seek" (v. 16), "bring back" (v. 16), "bind up" (v. 16), and "strengthen" His sheep (v. 16).[50] In the end, there can be no doubt that God will divinely care for His sheep.[51] The ultimate assurance that we have, on divine credit, is that God has and will care for His sheep. Stephen Rummage will address this aspect of the true Shepherd in chapter 10.

The Accountability of the Sheep

The second half of Ezekiel 34 reveals a final negative impact of the faithless shepherds. They were bad examples for the sheep. Not only were the shepherds abusing the sheep; the sheep were abusing one another. The sheep had taken on the characteristics of the shepherds. Thus, not only were there "wolves in wolves' clothing, but there . . . also [were] wolves in sheep's clothing."[52]

The results of the abuse afflicted by the sheep against other sheep paralleled those of the faithless shepherds—the sheep were scattered (34:20). Moreover, they, like the anti-shepherds, were also held accountable.

The obvious parallel to the work of the church is beyond the focus of this book. Not every lost sheep is the shepherd's fault. Some sheep are lost because of their own sin, and others are scattered because of exploitation by other sheep. Thus, the message is clear: shepherds must care for the sheep, and sheep must care for each other because the true Shepherd will hold them both accountable.

---

[50] See Chae, *Jesus as the Eschatological Davidic Shepherd*, 58. Chae notes a parallel in the "I will" statements of God in Ezek 34:13–17 and 20:34–35.

[51] See also Cooper, *Ezekiel*, 304–5 for a good discussion on the promises of the good Shepherd.

[52] Jefferson, *The Minister as Shepherd*, 36.

Provision for the Sheep (vv. 23–31)

The final section of Ezekiel 34 focuses on the messianic anticipation of the coming of the good Shepherd. This section reveals that someday the one true Shepherd will rule over all God's people. The coming of the one Shepherd will inaugurate a covenant of peace.[53] The explanation of this covenant corresponds with Jeremiah's prophecy of a new covenant (Jer 31:31–34).

In a similar way as the chapter began with a verdict against the shepherds, it ends with a pronouncement for the sheep. God climactically concludes with a fourfold message of assurance to His sheep, with the first two written in third person and the last two written in second person.[54] Verse 30 is a message from God to the prophet regarding the people. He told Ezekiel that when the good Shepherd reigns, then "they shall know that I, the LORD their God, am with them, and they, the house of Israel, are My people." Perhaps this message was as much for the prophet as it was for the people.

The final message of assurance is addressed by God directly to His people. Heretofore, God spoke to His people through His prophet. This message He wanted them to hear directly from Him. He closes the message with a personal word of affirmation, wanting them to be certain of their identity: "You are My flock, the flock of My pasture; you are men [i.e., human], and I am your God."

Those are the last words of God's message in Ezekiel 34 regarding the shepherds and the sheep. In them, we learn two things about God and two about His sheep:

- "I am with them." God promised to be with His sheep. Circumstances may shake us, but God's abiding presence sustains us.
- "They are My people." God wanted them to know that they are His. Though we may have wandered from the flock, He knows us and we belong to Him.

---

[53] Cp. Num 25:12; Isa 54:10; Ezek 37:26; Mal 2:5.
[54] Note this tense shift as a counter balance to the previous shift in verses 2 and 3.

- "You are My flock." God stamped His name upon them. The hireling may abandon the sheep in their need, but the divine Shepherd never abandons His flock.
- "I am your God." We are His flock—that is who we are. He is our God—that is who He is. Although human shepherds may fail to live up to their name, God always is faithful to His.

Those are words sheep and shepherds both need to hear.

The Ministry of a Shepherd

This book is addressed especially to church ministers and to those preparing for ministry positions. The purpose is not to propose a new strategy or recommend a new program. In fact, it is just the opposite. The point of this book is to present something God made clear over 2,500 years ago. He has made His intention known. The ministry of a shepherd has not changed.

If we are called by God, then we should do the work He desires to be done. More than hearing from the sheep, we need to listen to the true Shepherd. More than pursuing the felt needs of the needy, we must follow the established design of the Creator.

Pastor, God has told you in His Word what He expects from you. The responsibilities of your calling are clear. He expects His shepherds to feed the flock, strengthen the weak, heal the sick, bind up the broken, protect the flock, bring back those driven away, seek those lost, and lead the flock. This is where your calling begins. Whatever else you do must not be at the expense of what God said must be done.

Every minister should want to do the Lord's will. Even those who have ended poorly in ministry did not start out looking to fail. Somewhere along the way, they lost focus, forgot their calling, or started pursuing their own interests. This book is designed to help prevent that. Some shepherds are tired in the field. The needs of the sheep overwhelm, frustrate, and sometimes confuse them. This book has something for every shepherd. Others are burdened and questioning their calling. My prayer is that this book will encourage you and reaffirm God's desire for your life and ministry. If you are a new shepherd preparing for the responsibility of ministry, there is no better place to turn than the words of the Father outlining the duties of your calling. This is what God said you are to do. If God honors you with the care of His sheep, follow the ministry of the true Shepherd.

CHAPTER 2

Feed the Flock

David Allen

The Shepherd Analogy in Scripture

The shepherd motif is one of the pivotal analogies of Scripture. In the Old Testament, God Himself is the "shepherd" of His people Israel, signifying the tender relationship God established with them (Ps 23). Old Testament kings, priests, and prophets are often spoken of as "shepherds" of God's people (Isa 40:11; Ezek 34).

"Shepherd" is the personal analogy of Jesus in the Gospels and in Revelation. Jesus said, "I am the good shepherd" (John 10:11). In Rev 7:17, speaking of Jesus, John records: "For the Lamb who is in the midst of the throne will shepherd them and lead them to living fountains of waters."

"Shepherd" is the pastoral analogy used in Acts and the New Testament letters to describe the role of the pastor or elder in a local church (Acts 20:17–35; Eph 4:12; 1 Pet 5:1–4). Our English word *pastor* means "shepherd."

The early church drew upon this shepherd imagery. The Catacombs of Rome have drawings of shepherds on the walls. *The Shepherd of Hermas* was an important pastoral document in the early church. Christian hymnody also makes use of the shepherd analogy, as in the hymn "Savior Like a Shepherd Lead Us" by Dorothy Thrupp. In theological curricula today, the theological nomenclature used for pastoral ministry is *poimenics*, which derives from the Greek word in the New Testament for "shepherd" (*poimēn*).

The job of every faithful pastor is to tend the flock of God. This role involves many things, but none more important than feeding the flock a steady diet of the Word of God through preaching. A pastor is a preacher.

Paul, in his farewell address to the Ephesian elders in Acts 20:17–35, used the shepherd analogy to describe the pastoral role of the elders: "Therefore take heed to yourselves and to all the flock, among which the Holy Spirit has made you overseers, to shepherd the church of God which He purchased with His own blood" (v. 28). The Lord's church is a "flock," and the pastors are "shepherds" charged with the duty of caring for the flock. This duty of the pastor is the highest calling possible, made evident by the statement that the Lord's church was purchased with the blood of the great Shepherd, Jesus.

In 2 Timothy, after a statement concerning the inspiration of Scripture and the uses that pastors should make of it while preaching to the church (3:16), Paul passionately exhorts the young preacher Timothy, "Preach the word!" (4:2). At the end of Paul's last letter before his martyrdom, as he gives something of his "last words" to his young protégé, Paul indicates to Timothy and to us that the preaching of the word in the local church is paramount.

This same shepherd imagery appears in Jesus's postresurrection encounter with Simon Peter on the seashore (John 21). After providing the weary fishermen-disciples with breakfast, Jesus asked Peter a probing question: "Simon . . . , do you love Me . . . ?" When Peter responded in the affirmative, Jesus then said to him, "Feed My lambs" (v. 15). Jesus asked Peter the same question a second time. When Peter again responded in the affirmative, Jesus said, "Tend My sheep" (v. 16). A third time Jesus asked Peter the same question, and a third time Peter responded that he loved Jesus. Jesus then exhorted him a third time, "Feed My sheep" (v. 17).

The primary meaning of our Lord's threefold command to Peter has to do with Peter's preaching the Word of God. This preaching ministry of

Peter, and of all the disciples, would be for a twofold purpose: evangelism of the lost and edification of the saved. The preaching and teaching of the Word of God is foundational and fundamental for the health of the church.

Jesus's words to Peter marked his ministry for life. Peter exhorted the church elders, "Shepherd the flock of God which is among you" (1 Pet 5:1–4). This command is followed with several modifiers describing how to go about this sacred task, culminating with the words: "And when the Chief Shepherd appears, you will receive the crown of glory that does not fade away" (v. 4). Scripture makes clear that God's undershepherds must faithfully preach the Word.

Why is preaching so important? Why is it so vital that pastors preach the Bible faithfully to their people? Preaching is God's way of heralding the gospel to a lost world and of building up the church. Preachers have a twofold responsibility. They are responsible to God to preach His Word faithfully. And they are responsible to the church to feed God's flock.

Today's Lack of Biblical Preaching

Content

Yet, there is a dearth of genuine biblical preaching in many churches today. The church is anemic spiritually for many reasons, but one of the major reasons has to be the loss of biblical content in so much of contemporary preaching. Today's pulpits are filled with their share of curiosities, mediocrities, and atrocities. Much of the preaching that cascades over pulpits today is anything but an exposition of a text of Scripture. Eloquent nonsense abounds; sometimes it is not even eloquent. Doctrine is watered down either from neglect or from a willingness to compromise to attract people. Some preachers, instead of expounding the text, skirmish cleverly on its outskirts, pirouetting on trifles to the amazement of the congregation.

The Bible has been displaced by personal experience, pop psychology, and pragmatism packaged with "Five Ways to Be Happy" sermons. In the headlong rush to be relevant, *People* magazine, popular television shows, and other pop culture gadgets have replaced Scripture as sermonic resources. No wonder so many spiritual teeth are decaying in our churches. Today's sermonic focus, therefore, is on application. But application, without textual warrant for such, does not "stick"; it needs the glue of textual meaning. Accordingly, biblical content must precede application. How else can we possibly know what to apply?

Some preachers defend their lack of exposition of Scripture with the unfounded notion that exposition alone will not hold people's attention. The problem is not with exposition; the problem is with *boring* exposition! You can be creative and expository at the same time. But you must make sure that the creativity does not override the exposition. "Creativity" has become the word-of-the-day in preaching. I am all for creativity. But some preachers are allowing creativity to override the exposition of Scripture. Creativity without exposition is like a magic show where the preacher, with conjuring adroitness, pulls a fat rabbit out of an empty hat. Everybody "oohs" and "ahs," but they leave knowing that it was all an illusion—all show and no substance.

The crisis of preaching is also seen in the kinds of sermons that are preached, even in evangelical churches. In one interview a few years back, *Preaching* magazine asked a leading megachurch pastor, "Tell me about your use of Scripture in your sermons." He responded, "Everything we do comes from a biblical worldview and is according to scriptural principles. So, even if I'm preaching a topical series, I'm always in the Bible."

There is something vague about his answer. Making the statement that "it all comes from the Bible" attempts to place the various types of preaching—topical, textual, and expository—all on the same par in terms of faithfulness to the text and benefit to the church. I've heard many "topical series" that had little to do with the Bible. Topic-driven preaching is at least one step removed from what the text of Scripture actually says. Such preaching may be strong on application, but it is biblically weak. Topical preaching is preaching about the Bible. Expository preaching is preaching the Bible. There is a world of difference.

Do not get me wrong. I believe we should use all the tools in our homiletical toolbox to preach Scripture in a creative way and bring people in contact with Jesus. Let me be clear: I am not against the occasional use of PowerPoint, drama, props, and video clips; but do not let these detract from the main agenda, the verbal preaching of the Word of God by a

Spirit-filled man of God. If you cannot preach without the help of visual media, you will never be able to preach with it!

The sheer weightlessness, even overt heresy, of some preaching is astounding.[1] By what hubris do we think we could possibly have anything more important to say than what God Himself has said through Scripture? To substitute the words of men for the words of God is the height of arrogance. So much modern-day preaching is horizontal in dimension rather than vertical. Man-centered preaching strives to appeal to so-called felt needs instead of exalting God before the people as the One who alone can meet true and genuine needs.

Church Growth Movement

One of the culprits behind today's lack of biblical preaching is the Church Growth movement. Since its inception in America in 1971, the Church Growth movement has promised preachers success. Myriads of books have been written on the Church Growth movement. I have many of them in my own library. The influence of the Church Growth movement among the pastors and leaders of America's more than 400,000 evangelical and charismatic churches has been phenomenal. But the Church Growth movement has actually hindered preaching by de-emphasizing (either deliberately or by neglect) its importance in the local church. Have you ever

---

[1] This is illustrated in the book *What's the Matter with Preaching Today?*, ed. Mike Graves (Louisville: Westminster John Knox Press, 2004). This multiauthor book, which contains chapters by major homileticians in the nonevangelical mainline denominations, is nothing short of appalling at points. David Buttrick thinks the idea that Jesus saves individual human souls is a "heretical gospel" ("A Fearful Pulpit, a Wayward Land," 46). Ernest T. Campbell affirms his belief that Jesus is not necessarily the only way of salvation for people: "It is preposterous and indefensible to deny the possibility of salvation to the billions who share this planet with us but do not share our faith" ("A Lover's Quarrel with Preaching," 52). In another multiauthor book edited by homiletician Ronald J. Allen, *Patterns of Preaching: A Sermon Sampler* (St. Louis: Chalice Press, 1998), a chapter titled "Preaching in a Postmodern Perspective" includes a sermon on Phil 2:5–11 by John S. McClure ("Alienation > Emptying > Compassion"). McClure states that Christ emptied Himself of His desire to use His power for domination, to use others for His own ends. McClure further states that, being born in human likeness, "Jesus had no assurance that he could empty himself of these evil patterns of dominating power" (250). This is nothing short of a heretical Christology.

noticed how many of the Church Growth books talk about preaching? Precious few. Many of them do not even mention preaching.[2]

This de-emphasis is a result of the Church Growth movement's headlong desire to focus on marketing techniques, leadership styles, and creativity. Evangelicals may be outstripping everyone else as the supreme compromisers in church growth today. When you think about it, there is not much difference between a popular, market-driven philosophy of church growth and classical liberalism. Both have resulted in a compromise to culture. Classical liberalism capitulated to culture, and much of evangelicalism is compromising with culture. The evidence can be heard in sermons preached every Sunday morning.

God's shepherds should be very careful about collaborating with culture, especially when it comes to preaching. The gospel has always been countercultural. If you collaborate with the culture, you dilute the pure Word of the living Lord in the matter of preaching. An undefined theology, combined with a seeker-sensitive philosophy, undermines the ability of the church to speak prophetically to culture because the moment you defy the spirit of the age, you forfeit your marketing appeal.

The New Homiletic

Another culprit contributing to the dearth of biblical preaching in churches today is the New Homiletic. Interestingly, both the Church

---

[2] David Eby's *Power Preaching for Church Growth* (Fearn, Ross-shire, Scotland: Mentor, 1996) is one of the few books that deals with the subject of preaching and church growth. Eby notes that over 334 books on American church growth had been published as of 1996. He also points out that the Charles E. Fuller Institute of Evangelism and Church Growth had conducted 75 seminars annually with a total attendance of 15,000. The seminaries and Christian colleges offering courses on church growth are now too many to name. Eby went through every book in the Church Growth movement, read them, and charted where they talk about preaching. He first ransacked all of the early books and found only one of the first 16 books even listed biblical preaching as an aspect of church growth. He then ransacked the next 48 books that were published on church growth—over 10,000 pages—but fewer than 50 even mentioned preaching as important for church growth. Then Eby moved on to the Church Renewal movement, read more than 2,000 pages of print there, and found only passing references and 7 pages devoted to preaching in terms of how to grow a church—7 pages out of 2,000! Next, he examined all the doctor of ministry dissertations at Fuller Theological Seminary's library. Of the 377 DMin dissertations completed at Fuller since 1971, only *one* had been written on preaching and church growth.

Growth movement and the New Homiletic began in the same year: 1971. Fred Craddock's *As One Without Authority* was published that year and is recognized as the beginning of the New Homiletic movement in preaching.[3] Craddock championed *inductive* preaching as opposed to the more traditional *deductive* (i.e., "expository") model. The goal of preaching as he saw it was to create in the hearers an experience that would cause people to listen to the gospel. The New Homiletic is a paradigm shift from deductive to inductive, from left brain to right brain, from direct to indirect, from description to image. The goal of preaching shifts from the communication of information to the creation of an experience.

Furthermore, according to the New Homiletic, since human experience is inherently narrative, a sermon should be designed to be experienced and to create an experience rather than to assemble thoughts. Life is a story, so the best way to reach people in preaching is with lots of stories woven together around a single theme, which gradually will break in on the consciousness of the listener as the sermon progresses. Rather than following points given deductively in a sermon, the listeners draw their own conclusions about the text indirectly as they listen to the skillful interweaving of story with the text. A narrative sermon proceeds not by propositions and logical reasoning but is identified by its plot, which involves conflict: complication and rising tension, reversal, and then resolution.

These two key elements—(1) the rejection of expository preaching in favor of a narrative structure, and (2) the attempt to create an experience rather than communicate truth—are the twin pillars of the New Homiletic. Homiletician Thomas Long, summarizing the shift that has taken place in homiletics, notes that in the past, preaching sought to communicate meaning in a propositional way. Today, however, a fundamental axiom of most homileticians is that the audience and the preacher together create the experience of meaning.[4] Robert Reid, Jeffrey Bullock, and David Fleer have shown that the goal of the New Homiletic is to reach the will through

---

[3] Fred B. Craddock, *As One Without Authority*, rev. ed. (St. Louis: Chalice Press, 2001).
[4] Thomas G. Long, "And How Shall They Hear? The Listener in Contemporary Preaching," in *Listening to the Word: Studies in Honor of Fred B. Craddock*, ed. Gail R. O'Day and Thomas G. Long (Nashville: Abingdon Press, 1993), 167–88.

the imagination rather than through reason.[5] The privileging of individual experience of narrative and imagination over rational discourse is the essence of the New Homiletic.[6]

But there are serious problems, not the least of which is a thoroughly Barthian approach to biblical authority, which views Scripture as less than direct revelation from God. Such a view of Scripture makes one less prone to preach the Bible in an expositional fashion. A second problem is that there is sometimes precious little text found amidst the stories—and sometimes without enough content for people to connect the dots. Unless God tells us verbally what He is doing on the cross, we will miss the point of the story! The point is that, for the most part, the New Homiletic actually denigrates expository preaching.

Those who argue for narrative preaching claim that expository preaching does not increase the likelihood of the listeners experiencing God but rather makes this encounter less likely. "Exposition" may be a dirty word in homiletics today, but the fact is that you cannot "experience" someone fully without knowing something about that someone. The unnecessary wedge between "propositional" and "personal" has always been misplaced, whether you are talking about the nature of biblical revelation or preaching. Both are indispensable. You do not encounter God apart from His Word; you encounter God *through* His Word. You cannot separate God from His Word.

One should also think carefully about whether the medium can be separated from the message. Steven Smith aptly demonstrates the connection between God's truth and the method of text-driven preaching. If the job of the preacher is to expose people to God's revealed truth, then he must ask whether his method itself is text-driven. Does my sermon say about God what God says in the way God says it? Some preachers want to keep the message of the text but change the method of preaching in order to demonstrate the relevance of the message. The fundamental mistake here is that such a move underestimates the power of the method to become the

---

[5] Robert Reid, Jeffrey Bullock, and David Fleer, "Preaching as the Creation of an Experience: The Not-So-Rational Revolution of the New Homiletic," *JCR* 18, no. 1 (1995): 1–9.
[6] Ibid., 7.

message, as Marshal McLuhan affirms.[7] Some preachers act as if they do not believe in the power of the spoken word. They assume that the non-verbal is more effective in communicating than the verbal. All nonverbal communication must say what the text says in the way the text says it. Entertainment does not do this. Connecting with people alone does not do this.[8]

The Rod and the Staff: Text-Driven Preaching

If the Church Growth movement and the New Homiletic are insufficient foundations for text-driven preaching, in what kind of preaching should preachers engage? Since all pastors are under mandate to "Preach the word" (2 Tim 4:2), the nature of Scripture demands an expositional style of preaching. God is the ultimate author of all Scripture (2 Tim 3:16). All Scripture is God's speech. God and Scripture are used interchangeably when quoting the Old Testament. God is viewed as the author of Scripture even when He is not the direct speaker (e.g., Matt 19:4–5). The phrase "and God said" is used when God is the direct speaker (e.g., Gen 9:12). All Scripture is God's Word. In three passages, Paul personifies Scripture as God's speech (Rom 9:17; 10:11; Gal 3:8). What Scripture says is the Word of God. I like what J. I. Packer says: "Holy Scripture should be thought of as God preaching."[9] The first theological foundation for expository preaching is "God has spoken."

The power of preaching is not in the preacher's experience, opinions, creativity, or rhetorical skills but in God's powerful words. The preacher is the delivery boy. God writes the news. Only the written words of Scripture can give authority to your preaching (see the word "author" in "authority"). Biblical authority and expository preaching are so related that the loss of one ultimately leads to the loss of the other. Furthermore, the loss of expository preaching leads to diminished biblical content in the sermon.

---

[7] See "The Medium Is the Message," chapter 1 of Marshal McLuhan's influential book *Understanding Media* (New York: McGraw-Hill, 1964), 7–21.

[8] Steven W. Smith, *Dying to Preach: Embracing the Cross in the Pulpit* (Grand Rapids: Kregel, 2009), 46–55. This book should be read by every pastor!

[9] J. I. Packer, *God Has Spoken: Revelation and the Bible*, 3rd ed. (Grand Rapids: Baker, 1979, 1993), 91.

Consider Paul's approach in Thessalonica: he went in "a synagogue of the Jews . . . and for three Sabbaths reasoned with them from the Scriptures" (Acts 17:2). This account indicates use of some form of exposition. Look at the Pauline epistles, which are mostly written sermons. Look at the book of Hebrews, which is itself a sermon. The author explains the meaning of Scripture to the people and then makes application. Expository preaching fulfills the biblical mandate to preach the Word.

Many a sermon uses a text but is not derived from the text. The text of such a sermon is not its source; it is only a resource. The text of Scripture should be the message, not a footnote to it. Biblical inspiration and authority mandate that Scripture has the right to determine both the substance and the structure of the sermon. Since the term "expository preaching" has been stretched beyond the breaking point in some cases, I prefer the term *text-driven preaching* to describe the kind of expositional preaching pastors should be doing. Every text has a certain structure to it. That structure communicates the meaning the author desires to convey to his audience. Every text has mainline information that is semantically dominant and background information that is semantically subordinate. The faithful shepherd/preacher, through careful exegesis, must determine this structure and then follow its lead in sermon preparation.

Text-driven preaching is not enslaved to artificial outlining techniques, such as a three-point structure and alliteration. "Expository preaching" is a broad umbrella term that permits a wide variety of styles and structures to communicate the meaning of the text. The text-driven preacher strives to practice exposition not imposition. Faulty hermeneutical methods such as spiritualizing and allegorizing the text are avoided. The preacher's goal is to allow the text to stand forth in all its uniqueness and power. Text-driven preaching is driven by the text, not by theology. Theology serves the text, not the other way around. First, the text, then theology. Biblical theology therefore precedes systematic theology. Text-driven preachers also believe that creativity ultimately resides in the text itself. The first place to look for creativity to employ in preaching is often the last place that many preachers look—the text itself. All the creativity in the world is of no value if the text itself is neglected, obscured, or ignored in the process of preaching. Genuine biblical preaching recognizes an inextricable link between the text of Scripture and the sermon preached. Exegesis is the preliminary task of the preacher. To succeed in text-driven preaching, one must delight in exegetical study of the Bible, in searching out the exact meaning of its paragraphs, sentences, phrases, and words. Knowledge of the original languages of Scripture, while not indispensable, is highly recommended. God's faithful shepherds who pastor local churches should "preach the word." To preach effectively will require lots of time in preparation. Shamefully, more than 90 percent of pastors in America spend only two hours per week in sermon preparation for each message preached.[10] To accomplish everything that needs to be done in good sermon preparation in merely two hours per week is virtually impossible.

Preachers must consider the *then* and the *now* in preaching. Preaching is giving contemporary expression of a text to make it understandable. Only when the sermon is preached can the meaning of the text be translated into the contemporary context of an audience in terms they understand.[11] Text-driven shepherds refuse to let the flock walk away without understanding what God is saying to them through the text. People encounter God *through* the text of Scripture, not outside the text of Scripture. Jesus said to the disciples on the road to Emmaus, "'O foolish ones, and slow of heart to believe in all that the prophets have spoken! Ought not the Christ to have suffered these things and to enter into His glory?' And beginning at Moses and all the Prophets, He expounded to them in all the Scriptures the things concerning Himself" (Luke 24:25–27).

Senseless Shepherds and Scattered Sheep

In 627 BC, a young priest in Israel heard God's call to be a prophet. The ministry of Jeremiah—who was born in Anathoth, three miles northeast of Jerusalem—spanned 40 turbulent years. He witnessed firsthand the death of his nation. His king, Josiah, had come to the throne 15 years earlier at the tender age of eight. Josiah's wicked father, Amon, ruled only

---

[10] Thom S. Rainer, *Surprising Insights from the Unchurched and Proven Ways to Reach Them* (Grand Rapids: Zondervan, 2001), 67.

[11] Thomas W. Gillespie, "Biblical Authority and Interpretation: The Current Debate on Hermeneutics," in *The Bible in Theology and Preaching*, ed. Donald K. McKim (Eugene, OR: Wipf & Stock, 1999), 195–96.

two years before being assassinated at the age of 24. When Josiah was 16, he began to seek the Lord (2 Chr 34:3). Through a series of spiritual reforms, he temporarily turned some of the nation from idolatry back to the Lord. But the revival under Josiah was to be short-lived. He died in 609 BC, killed by the Egyptian army at the valley of Megiddo. From that day till now, Jews have regarded this event as a decisive turning point of a lost battle and lost righteousness. Four years later (605 BC), it was bag-packing time for those in Jerusalem as the first deportation to Babylon occurred under the cruel Nebuchadnezzar. The southern kingdom was coming to an end.

Throughout this time of national upheaval, Jeremiah preached the Word of God. For the most part, the leaders and people rejected his preaching. Jeremiah suffered because the leaders of his nation and his temple were incompetent and ungodly. They had led the nation into idolatry. Listen to his indictment:

> For the shepherds have become dull-hearted,
> And have not sought the LORD;
> Therefore they shall not prosper,
> And all their flocks shall be scattered." (Jer 10:21)

The "shepherds" are the spiritual leaders, including the king, the priests, and the prophets. "Have become dull-hearted" reflects Jeremiah's stunning use of the Hebrew word *ba'ar*, meaning "become stupid, senseless"—i.e., like an animal, which is deficient in moral and spiritual things. It refers to those who do not fear the Lord or desire His wisdom; consequently, they are senseless and stupid. Jeremiah would agree with Forrest Gump: "Stupid is as stupid does."[12]

But how did this remarkable condition occur? Israel's spiritual leaders became stupid because they did not "seek" (Hb. *darash*) the Lord. This word is the focal point of the verse. It occurs 165 times in the Old

---

[12] Gump is the main character in the motion picture *Forrest Gump*, directed by Robert Zemeckis (1994; Los Angeles: Paramount Pictures); screenplay by Eric Roth, based on the novel by Winston Groom. See http://www.dailyscript.com/scripts/forrest_gump.html.

Testament, mostly in the sense of seeking after the Lord. It means "to seek with intensity and with care."[13]

Three primary aspects are observed in the various contextual uses of this word. All three can be seen in Ezra 7:10: "For Ezra had prepared his heart to seek [*darash*] the Law of the LORD. . . ." First, there is the volitional aspect of the word. One does not accidentally seek God. Seeking him is an act of the will. Second, there is an emotional aspect to the word: "Ezra prepared his heart to seek" (cp. Ps 119:10, "With my whole heart I have sought [*darash*] You"). Third, there is an intellectual aspect to the word. Ezra set his heart to "seek" (*darash*)—i.e., to study—"the Law of the Lord." Israel's leaders sought God's will first through the prophets, then later through the written Word of God. Isaiah 34:16 says, "Search [*darash*] from the book of the LORD." The word in Ezra 7:10 denotes the element of "research, investigation, study." *Darash* is regularly used for discovering the mind of God (Deut 4:29; 12:5; Isa 31:1; Hos 10:12; Amos 5:4–6).

This insight is important for preachers. The fundamental way you seek the Lord is by seeking Him in His Word, the Scriptures. Some preachers today are seeking God *apart* from His Word. There are some in the Charismatic movement who say God speaks today in new revelations in addition to the Bible. Here is the problem for preaching, as I see it; such an approach diverts attention from Scripture. People are looking for a *new* word; and without the grounding of Scripture, they are liable to get something that is not from God at all.[14]

---

[13] On this word, consult Siegfried Wagner, "דָּרַשׁ *dārash [dāraš]*," in *TDOT*, ed. G. Johannes Botterweck and Helmer Ringgren (Grand Rapids: Eerdmans, 1978), 3:293–307; R. Laird Harris, Gleason L. Archer Jr., and Bruce K. Waltke, *TWOT* (Chicago: Moody, 1980), 1:198–99; G. Gerleman and E. Ruprecht, "דרשׁ *drš*," in *TLOT*, ed. Ernst Jenni and Claus Westermann (Peabody, MA: Hendrickson, 1997), 1:346–51; and Willem A. VanGemeren, ed., trans. Mark E. Biddle, *NIDOTTE* (Grand Rapids: Zondervan, 1997), 1:993–99.

[14] Hank Hanegraaff, in his book *Counterfeit Revival* (Orange, CA: W. Publishing Group, 2001), recounts the story of Pastor James Ryle who during his sermon spotted a lady in his congregation with the cartoon character Olive Oyl superimposed on her face. Apparently Ryle was the only one who could see the image and he interpreted it as a sign from God. He then offered this interpretation. Like Olive Oyl, the lady was being fought over by a "Bluto" and "Popeye had come to the rescue." Ryle then turned the word "Popeye" into a pun, saying that the woman was the "apple of the Father's eye"—"Pop's Eye" (82–83).

Jeremiah is preeminently the prophet of the "Word." Almost half of the occurrences of the phrase "thus says the LORD" appear in Jeremiah. To understand that the Old Testament emphasizes meeting God in His spoken and written Word is fundamentally important.

Note the urgency and intensity in Ezra 7:10: he "prepared his heart to seek." Also notice the ethical obligation that follows from studying the law: "to do it." The act of *darash*, "studying," is completed only with the practicing of what is "studied or sought." The act of "seeking" contains an element of activity—action and energy—and is completed only with the practicing of that which is sought. Notice the order: to study, to do, and to teach. You cannot do it until you study it, and you cannot preach it until you study it and do it! Some preachers are trying to "preach" it without studying it or doing it! Interestingly, the modern Hebrew word for preaching (*darshanut*) is a form of the word *darash*. To study the Word, prepare the sermon, and preach it all intertwine in this word *darash*.

In Jer 10:21, two consequences follow from not "seeking" the Lord. First, the shepherds "shall not prosper." The Hebrew word is *sakal,* which denotes the process of thinking through a complex arrangement of thoughts resulting in wise action and use of practical common sense, the end result of which is success. But in 10:21, the shepherds will have no success. In fact, all their flocks will be "scattered" (Hb. *puts*), a favorite word of Jeremiah. *The Message* translates 10:21 this way:

It's because our leaders are stupid.
They never asked God for counsel.
And so nothing worked right.
The people are scattered all over.[15]

Failure to "seek" the Lord and to "study" the Word leads to a threefold loss: a personal loss (senseless preachers), a professional loss (they have not prospered), and a pastoral loss (scattered sheep). The problem with some preaching today is that too many of God's shepherds are not

---

[15] Eugene H. Peterson, *The Message: The Bible in Contemporary Language* (Colorado Springs: NavPress, 2002).

"seeking" the Lord in the study of the Word and then feeding that Word to the flock.

Ezekiel 34 is God's powerful indictment against the false shepherds of Israel. Here God preaches against the preachers! In verses 2–3, God says: "Son of man, prophesy against the shepherds of Israel, prophesy and say to them, 'Thus says the Lord GOD to the shepherds: "Woe to the shepherds of Israel who feed themselves! Should not the shepherds feed the flock?"'" Verse 5 reveals the negligence of the false shepherds in failing to care for the flock. In verses 9–10, God says: "[T]herefore O shepherds, hear the word of the LORD! Thus says the Lord GOD: 'Behold, I am against the shepherds, and I will require [*darash*] My flock at their hand.'" Whereas the false shepherds refused to "seek" [*darash*] the Lord and the Lord's flock who had gone astray, God Himself as the Shepherd of Israel searches for [*darash*] His sheep. God's shepherds are responsible to God both for what they committed against the sheep and for what they omitted.

To seek the Lord involves three things: prayer, studying the Word, and preaching the Word. Sheep need a pastor who seeks the Lord—i.e., who is a praying preacher, a studying preacher, and a preaching preacher. Spiritual shepherds are to govern the flock gently, protect them constantly, provide for them carefully, feed them faithfully, and seek them diligently. Because the false shepherds failed in their duty, God said: "And I will give you shepherds according to My heart, who will feed you with knowledge and understanding" (Jer 3:15).

The false shepherds in Jeremiah's day offered people visual images instead of the Word of the Lord. An idol is visible, but it is not real. Idolatry is the quintessence of virtual reality—an image-based worship. The first case of idolatry in Israel occurred when Moses returned with the Ten Commandments and found the people worshiping a golden calf. Think of the difference: a golden calf (an image) on one hand and the Ten Commandments (God's Word) on the other. The second of those commandments prohibits the making of any "image" (Exod 20:4).

Much of today's preaching offers people virtual reality, not reality. If you watch sports on television, you may have noticed all of the billboard advertisements on the field. What you probably did not notice is that the advertisement logos you see on television have been digitally superimposed to cover up what is actually on those billboards. The networks sell advertising and then superimpose the company name of the advertiser over the *real* advertisement on the field. The networks restructure your reality for their own profit. In similar fashion, some preaching today is an attempt to restructure spiritual reality for the preacher's own profit. We superimpose our images over the real message of the Word of God.

Josiah started a spiritual reformation in Judah, which was a return to the Word of God. He began to tear down the idols. The revival that occurred in Josiah's day was Word-based. A rediscovery of the Word brought revival and the destruction of idols. He destroyed the virtual reality, the idols, in order to give people back true reality, God and His Word.

The difference between the Renaissance and the Reformation is that one was image-based and the other was Word-based. The Renaissance was a return to pagan Rome with its idols. The Reformation was a return to first-century Christianity with the preaching of the Word. Today postmodernism is primarily image-based. It is a turning away from rational discourse to image. Some today want to do the same with preaching. The idea of a man standing to preach the Word to listening people is outdated. Drama, props, video clips, and clever gimmicks replace the simple exposition of the Word. A culture enamored with image is an idolatrous culture. Preaching that is enamored with image, crowding out the verbal Word of the living God, is idolatrous preaching. If you cannot preach without all these things, then you will never be able to preach with them. When it comes to preaching, visual must never override verbal. Nothing should override the expositional preaching of the Word of God.

Text-driven preaching done right will stimulate an encounter with God that will be life-transforming. The experience is evoked *through* the content of the text, not *around* it. Fellowship with Jesus is "textually mediated." In preaching, we come face to face with the living Word, Jesus, when we are confronted with His written Word, the Scriptures. Experiencing God *does not work apart from textual content but through it.* Obedience to the written Word of God is a means of encounter and fellowship with Jesus, the living Word of God.

Preaching as Pastoral Care

Throughout church history, preaching has been viewed as the primary method of pastoral care. Listen to Martin Luther:

> If anybody wants to preach, let him suppress his own words . . . here in the church he should speak nothing but the Word . . . otherwise, it is not the true church. This is why it must always be said that it is God who is speaking. . . . Therefore a preacher . . . dare not say anything different from what God says and commands. And even though there may be a lot of talk which is not the Word of God, the church is not in all this talk, even though they begin to yell like mad.[16]

For Luther, preaching is the cure of souls; a vital way of pastoral care. Wayne Grudem is right on target:

> Throughout the history of church . . . , preaching has drawn its power not from the proclamation of . . . [the preachers'] own experiences or . . . opinions, creativity, or rhetorical skills, but from God's powerful words. Essentially they stood in the pulpit, pointed to the biblical text, and said in effect to the congregation, "This is what this verse means. Do you see that meaning here as well? Then you must believe it and obey it with all your heart, for God himself, your Creator and your Lord, is saying this to you today!" Only the written words of Scripture can give this kind of authority to preaching.[17]

Only eternity will identify who the great preachers are. You are going to be surprised at who receives the crown for faithful preaching in heaven. Many a man, unknown and unsung in this world, who faithfully preached the Bible, expounding it to his little church of 25 or 50, week in and week

---

[16] Martin Luther, "Sermon in Castle Pleissenburg, Leipzig, 1539," in *Luther's Works*, vol. 51, *Sermons: 1*, ed. and trans. John W. Doberstein (Philadelphia: Muhlenberg Press, 1959), 305.

[17] Wayne Grudem, *Systematic Theology: An Introduction to Biblical Doctrine* (Grand Rapids: Zondervan, 1994), 82.

out, will hear his name called by the Master before the throngs of heaven: "Well done, good and faithful servant."

May God raise up His shepherds, pastors who seek the Lord through the faithful study and exposition of Scripture and who will lead many to the Great Shepherd, Jesus. "And he who has My word, let him speak My word faithfully" (Jer 23:28).

CHAPTER 3

Strengthen the Weak

Deron J. Biles

Y ou have not strengthened the weak, healed the sick, bandaged the injured, brought back the strays, or sought the lost. Instead, you have ruled them with violence and cruelty" (Ezek 34:4).

King David is most often associated with strength. The stories of his defeat of Goliath, establishment of the kingdom, building of the city of Jerusalem, and the stories of his mighty men are renowned. However, David was also a man of great weakness.[1] At arguably the weakest moment of his career, David met one of his strongest champions.

On one occasion, David was fleeing the city of Jerusalem to avoid a potential civil war with his son Absalom, who was attempting a mutinous revolt against him. Second Samuel 15 records David's escape from the city and his seeming abdication of the throne (v. 19). The Bible notes that as David and his men retreated from the city, they stopped at the outskirts of the city to assess who was with David.

The author recounts the lineup of David's servants, then his special forces (the Cherethites and Pelethites), and finally a group of 600 Gittites

---

[1] See Deron J. Biles, *A Man After God's Heart: Becoming the Man God Is Seeking* (Denver: Outskirts Press, 2009), 4–6. Here, I argue that Scripture records more sins of David than of any other person.

and their families led by Ittai, passing before the true king.[2] This last group comprised an interesting addition to David's entourage. The Gittites came from Gath, one of the five major Philistine cities. One can imagine that Ittai and his men grew up hearing stories of David's defeat of their Philistine hero, Goliath.

Ittai's commitment to David was even more impressive when David acknowledged that Ittai had joined forces with him only 24 hours before the king fled the capital. Upon seeing Ittai, David offered him a no-shame excuse to leave. In fact, he even presented compelling reasons why Ittai should not follow him (2 Sam 15:19–20).

Ittai's response recalls the words of Ruth to Naomi (Ruth 1:16–17): "As the LORD lives, and as my lord the king lives, surely in whatever place my lord the king shall be, whether in death or life, even there also your servant will be" (2 Sam 15:21). Ittai was absolutely committed, regardless of what might happen, to following David wherever he led and whatever the circumstances. His promise to be with David was symbolized by the meaning of his name. Ittai in Hebrew means "with me," and that is what Ittai promised the king—his presence. David never had to wonder where Ittai was. Ittai was with him.

Later, in 2 Samuel 18, Ittai was true to his word. He was still with David, only with increased responsibility. David came to realize the value of Ittai's presence with him.

Everyone needs someone like Ittai. David valued Ittai for his leadership (he brought 600 men with him) and for his commitment: (1) Ittai was a foreigner away from home; (2) he and all his people brought their families with them; (3) he had just come the day before but was willing to leave with David imediately; and (4) he promised to stay with David, whether in life or death. We also recognize the timeliness of God's provision. God brought Ittai into David's life exactly when the king needed him. When David was weak, God brought someone into his life who could help make him strong. That is a function God also expects of His shepherds.

---

[2] See Francis Brown, "יָד," in BDBG (Peabody, MA: Hendrickson Publishers, 1979), 391. The phrase al-yad (עַל־יָד) in Scripture can mean "next to," "on hand," "by the side of," or even "under one's guidance" (i.e., 1 Chr 25:2).

The richness of God's instructions to the shepherds in Ezekiel 34 is that they convey the Chief Shepherd's expectations. The focus of this book is to examine the functions of a shepherd based on the standards for which God holds them accountable. This chapter will consider God's instruction to strengthen the weak. This particular expectation is the first of five functions highlighted in Ezek 34:4. Because of the unique guidelines in 34:4, this chapter will begin with a discussion of pastoral care, followed by a challenge to implement it in the church today. Next, the specific instruction to strengthen the weak will be examined. This will be done by analyzing the specific Hebrew word for weakness used in Ezek 34:4, followed by a general discussion of weakness throughout the Old and New Testaments and the Hebrew and Greek terms used to convey it. The purpose is to identify in Scripture the weak who must be strengthened. Finally, the chapter will conclude with biblical instructions on how to strengthen the weak.

Shepherds Care for the Sheep

Shepherding is varicolored and multifaceted. Even when we have said all we know to say about the ministry of a shepherd, much more could yet be said. Fundamentally, shepherds and care are indivisible. Noticeably, five of the eight functions of a shepherd described in Ezekiel 34 relate to pastoral care. Equally significant, these pastoral care functions are distinguishable by their individual, as opposed to corporate, applications.

The first function of a shepherd addressed in Ezekiel 34 is feeding. This activity is intended to reach all the flock. However, five of the next seven responsibilities that God outlines target specific subgroups within the flock (the weak, the sick, the broken, those driven away, and the lost). Thus, some of our shepherding functions are directed toward the whole flock (feeding, protecting, and leading), while others target sheep with specific needs.

The focus on weakness in Ezek 34:4 makes an interesting juxtaposition to the focus on feeding in 34:2–3—two different kinds of shepherding functions. In one sense, they represent the difference between preaching and pastoral care. Both categories are important, and we dare not neglect one to focus exclusively on the other.

Most people primarily associate the role of a pastor with preaching. Among laypeople, the question is often raised as to what a pastor does "the other six days of the week." Certainly, preaching, although a vital part of shepherding, is not the pastor's only function. Indeed, feeding the sheep is more glamorous than his other functions. Giving strength to the weak, on the other hand, requires a different skill set on the part of the shepherd. One can feed en masse from a distance, but one only strengthens up close and one at a time.

A Call to Pastoral Care

In all of Scripture, Ezekiel 34:4 provides the clearest picture of the responsibilities of pastoral care. Here, God outlines five aspects—strengthening, healing, binding, bringing back, and seeking—that address particular needs of specific sheep. These are not merely five hypothetical functions but represent actual needs of sheep. Shepherds do not function in a vacuum. They minister to real exigencies of sheep. The identification of and faithful ministry to those sheep with unique needs in our flocks defines our roles as shepherds.

Ezekiel 34:4 is a call to pastoral care. We cannot read this verse with integrity and sit by idly while the sheep suffer. It is time for pastors and churches to make a renewed commitment to an Ezek 34:4 ministry in the church.

What Is Pastoral Care?

Pastoral care is not synonymous with pastoral ministry. One is a subset of the other, but they are not the same any more than a kitchen is the same as the whole house.[3] William A. Clebsch and Charles R. Jaekle have effectively distinguished pastoral care from other related disciplines. They

---

[3] Sometimes, we become lazy in our use of terms in ministry. But, words have meaning. If we are not careful in our expression, we even allow the misuse of a word or phrase to become synonymous with the correct usage of it. For example, how many times have you heard the phrase "I could not care less" used synonymously with "I could care less," a phrase that actually denotes the complete opposite of what most people mean when they say it?

explain the functions of pastoral care as sustaining, guiding, healing, and reconciling.[4] These words effectively convey the work of pastoral care and fit precisely within Ezek 34:4. These functions are intended to be administered to the weak, sick, broken, driven away, and lost among God's sheep.

Identifying the functions of the care expected of shepherds is helpful, but pastoral care is never just theory. The "what" of pastoral care is meaningless without the perspective of the "who." The functions are only effective as they are administered in context. The shepherds indicted in Ezek 34:4 were held accountable for care that they did not administer—i.e., not just for missed opportunities but for failed obligations. Pastoral care is impotent outside of its context.

The Commitment to Pastoral Care

Every day, they are all around you—the needy, the poor, the outcast, and the downcast. You pass by them so often that you have become pretty adept at not even seeing them. Worse, that calloused attitude sometimes even invades the church. But, Ezek 34:4 admonishes that we must not look away; we have no excuse. We cannot be like the priest and Levite and pass by on the other side.

Pastoral care is definitely hard work. It is unglamorous, unrewarding (from a material perspective), and it often goes unnoticed or even unappreciated. But neglecting pastoral care is incongruous with being a shepherd. This chapter calls for a renewed commitment to pastoral care.

In Matt 25:31–46, Jesus announces the judgment of the sheep and goats. I find it interesting that in castigating the goats on His left, Jesus does not indict them for what they have done (as numerous as those infractions might have been). Rather, Jesus holds them accountable for what they have not done. As He unpacks the list of those to whom the goats have not ministered, it becomes clear that the ones not served were the weak.

---

[4] William A. Clebsch and Charles R. Jaekle, *Pastoral Care in Historical Perspective* (Northvale, NJ: Jason Aronson, 1994), xi. While I am indebted to Clebsch and Jaekle for effectively defining pastoral care and distinguishing it from pastoral ministry, they later blur the lines when they describe these functions as "the four pastoral functions" (32). The work would have been more consistent if they had continued to refer to these as the "functions of pastoral care" as they do on page 8.

They were the forgotten ones—those requiring ministry that typically is unrecognized and costly.

Jesus's indictment of the goats in Matt 25:31–46 parallels God's judgment of the shepherds in Ezekiel 34. The unconvincing protest of the goats, "Lord, if we had known it was you," merely emphasizes the fact that they had missed the point.[5] The goats, unconscious of their hardheartedness, seem shocked by the realization that they might be judged for their omission.

Indeed, even the response of the goats—"Lord, when did we *see* You hungry or thirsty or a stranger or naked or sick or in prison . . . ?"— convicted them (Matt 25:44, italics added for emphasis). The question revealed the heart of their problem: they did not see the weak. Is this not the problem of so many pastors today? Somehow, in all our business and despite all our busyness, we simply fail to *see* the weak.[6]

A similar application is found in the parable of the Good Samaritan (Luke 10:25–37). A lawyer asked Jesus what he needed to do to inherit eternal life. Jesus told him to love God and love his neighbor—the two things he had perhaps missed from the law. The lawyer wanted to justify himself so he probed further, "Who is my neighbor?" Jesus responded with a parable that highlighted a Samaritan who helped a man unable to help himself. Then, Jesus told the lawyer to do the same. Thus, loving the vulnerable by serving them is an indication of those who have the eternal life about which the lawyer had asked.

Such love is the heart of a faithful shepherd. It is the burden that causes him to move past the strategically important people to the needy ones. It is the love of the shepherd that keeps him up at night and alert during the day. It is what energizes his mind and compels his hands to serve the otherwise unnoticed, to attend unrelentingly to those under his care before the night comes when no man can work.

---

[5] Helmut Thielicke, "Forgive Us Our Debts," *Our Heavenly Father: Sermons on the Lord's Prayer*, trans. John W. Doberstein (New York: Harper & Brothers, 1960), 94–95.

[6] The Hebrew word for "shepherd" (*raʿah*) is a homophone of the Hebrew verb "to see" (*raʾah*). Certainly the functions of a shepherd require him to see the needs of the sheep. Thus, the shepherd (*raʿah*) must see (*raʾah*) the sheep.

In Ezekiel 34, the shepherds were going blithely on their way, never stopping to see the needs of the weak sheep around them. Thus, their undone deeds convicted them, as ours convict us. Shepherds must care for the sheep.

Shepherds and Pastoral Care

Ezekiel 34:4 emphasizes four truths about shepherds and pastoral care. First, it reveals the responsibility of the shepherd for pastoral care. The difficulty and lack of glamour in the task cannot mitigate the responsibility. To be sure, few may notice when you visit a widow in a nursing home, and the dividends of your care may not always match the effort inherent in them. But the shepherd's task is not defined by what gets noticed or rewarded. Your default must be to servanthood, and your standard must be faithfulness; to the end that we, like Jeremiah, can stand before God and declare, "I have not hurried away from being a shepherd who follows You" (Jer 17:16).

Second, Ezek 34:4 emphasizes the competence of the shepherd for pastoral care. Certainly, having a God-given responsibility to strengthen the weak implies the ability to do so. I believe that God equips those whom He has called for the ministries to which He has called them. However, that does not mean that you and I should not aggressively seek to improve our ability to shepherd throughout the lifetime of our ministries. Becoming competent may demand that we acquire or hone certain skills to accomplish the tasks entrusted to us.

This expectation of competence is one of the reasons I am a strong proponent of seminary education. That period of training for a minister is more than the accumulation of information. It is a time of preparation. It is the commitment to invest in your calling. Paige Patterson said, "There is not a 'fact' associated with the gospel that cannot be learned online or in the crucible of a church ministry; but the ripening of the soul, which is the product of vigorous study in a classroom of one's peers, the injustices sometimes experienced, and the companionship of the called are irreplaceable."[7] If God

---

[7] Paige Patterson, "Convocation Fall 2015" (video of sermon, Southwestern Baptist Theological Seminary Chapel, August 27, 2015), http://media.swbts.edu/item/1106/.

has called you to the ministry of a shepherd, He has called you to the ministry of preparation. We prepare today for the needs of the sheep God entrusts
to us tomorrow.

Third, Ezek 34:4 reveals that pastoral care requires the shepherd's
awareness of the needs of the sheep. Proverbs 27:23 says, "Be diligent to
know the state of your flocks." That is the responsibility of every shepherd.
We must be attentive to the needs of the sheep, and we dare not become so
preoccupied with the strong and vocal sheep that we forget about the weak
and silent ones.

Most pastors can relate stories of frustration when church members
became sick or went to the hospital without his knowledge. But that does
not seem to be the point of this passage. Rather, this text emphasizes the
responsibility of shepherds to be able to identify those who are in need and
to know the difference between one need and another. Among the many
things Paul may have been saying in 2 Cor 11:29 ("Who is weak and I am
not weak?"), his rhetorical question certainly reveal his awareness of the
Corinthian believers' weaknesses and how they affected him.

A fourth truth of pastoral care from Ezek 34:4 is the compassion of the
shepherd for the sheep. Mark notes that Jesus looked at the people and had
compassion for them, lamenting that "they were like sheep not having a
shepherd" (Mark 6:34).[8] Christ's compassion is the model of a shepherd's
care. The callous shepherd fails not for his ignorance but for his lack of
caring.

Thus, the call to pastoral care is an identification of the responsibility,
the competence, the awareness, and the compassion required for the ministry of a shepherd. In Ezekiel 34, this call was from God to the shepherds.
The groups described were to be the objects of the shepherd's care. "The
weak" were the first such group to be identified.

Shepherds to the Weak

In the same way that Jesus described categories of people who were
weak or vulnerable in Matthew 25 (hungry, thirsty, stranger, poor, sick, and
in prison), James described ministry to orphans and widows as reflecting

---

[8] See also Num 27:17; 1 Kgs 22:17; 2 Chr 18:16; Isa 13:14; Matt 9:36.

"pure and undefiled religion" (Jas 1:27). They were those whose circumstances caused them to be weak.

In Ezek 34:4, God outlines the groups to whom He expects shepherds to administer care: the weak, the sick, the broken, the driven away, and the lost. These five groups are, in one sense, set apart from the hungry (34:2), the unprotected (34:5, 8), and those who have not been led (34:5–6). The first two groups in need of the pastoral care depicted in 34:4 are described using two forms of the same Hebrew verb. They are "the weak" (Hb. *chalah*) and "those who were sick" (Hb. *chalah*). Throughout the Old Testament, *chalah* is used to describe both sickness and weakness,[9] often the latter a result of the former.

The word "chalah" (חָלָה) occurs 130 times in the Old Testament. Of those, 18 refer to a person's name[10] and one refers to a title of a psalm.[11]

God has taken a word that normally describes a condition (weakness or sickness) and used it to represent two groups of people. He charges the shepherds with having failed to minister to "the weak" and "the sick."

Since the same Hebrew word is used in 34:4 for both sickness and weakness, one must determine the word's meaning through its usage and context in order to distinguish between the two groups. The first use of *chalah* in 34:4 pairs weakness with strength.[12] The shepherds were being indicted for not strengthening the weak. Similarly, the second use of this

---

[9] When this word occurs in noun form in Hebrew, it almost always (35 out of 37 times) is rendered in English as some form of sickness. When the word in Hebrew is in the form of a verb, the translation is influenced by the tense of the verb. Normally, when the verb is in the Qal form (25 out of 37 occurrences) or Hithpael (3 out of 3 times), the word is rendered as some form of sickness. When the word occurs in the Piel form, it is almost always (16 out of 17 occurrences) rendered as "entreaty." Finally, when the Niphal (9 out of 9 times), Hiphil (3 out of 4 times), Hophal (3 out of 3 times), or Pual (1 out of 1) stems are employed, the word almost always connotes a form of weakness. In Ezek 34:4, the first occurrence of the word is in the Niphal stem, while the second is a Qal. Moreover, as is the case in Ezek 34:4, the context of the passage generally reveals the usage of the term to denote either weakness or sickness.

[10] The title to Psalm 5 is variously translated. The Hebrew phrase *hannechilot* (לוֹת הַנְּחִי) is often rendered "flute," from the Hebrew, *chalil* (חָלִיל). However, see HALOT, s.v. "נְחִילוֹת"; the word may also derive from *chalah* (חָלָה), which would convey an idea of sickness or weakness.

[11] See footnote 9, above.

[12] In the second use of the word in Ezek 34:4, sickness is paired with healing. This will be discussed in the next chapter.

word pairs sickness with healing. Thus, the distinction between the weak and sick becomes clear by what the Lord expected to have been done for them. The first group must be strengthened, and the second group must be healed.

The word "strong" functions in two ways in the sentence. First, it clarifies the translation of the word *chalah*. The translation of the word "weak" is understood because of the usage of the word "strong." Shepherds are to make the weak sheep strong. Second, the word "strong" in this verse explains the extent of the ministry that God expects the shepherds to fulfill for the sheep. Shepherds are to make them strong. They are not just to identify sheep as weak, commiserate with them, feel sorry for them, or even do small things for them. They are to make them strong. Thus, our ministry to weak sheep is not finished until they are strong.

Throughout the Old Testament, *chalah* is used in several ways. When it is used to describe the condition of weakness, *chalah* conveys either physical or mental weaknesses.[13] The weakness may be a result of vulnerability, injury, grief, or other circumstances.[14] Another use of this term describes weakness through sympathy or entreaty.[15] Thus, weakness is a consequence. The cause of this effect may or may not be apparent.

"The weak" described by God in Ezekiel 34 are not those outside the flock but those inside the flock. This does not mean that we do not minister to the weak who may be outside of the flock, but it does emphasize the responsibility to those within. These weak sheep had not left the flock, but neither had they been made strong.

Absent from the text is any mention of the sheep's awareness of their own weaknesses. Undoubtedly, some were aware of their needs,

---

[13] Deut 29:22; Judg 16:7, 11, 17; 1 Sam 22:8; 1 Kgs 22:34; 2 Kgs 1:2; 8:29; 2 Chr 18:33; 35:23; Prov 13:12; 23:35; Ecc 5:13, 16; 6:2; Isa 14:10; 53:3–4, 10; 57:10; Jer 4:31; 5:3; 12:13; Ezek 34:21; Dan 8:27; Amos 6:6; Mic 6:13.

[14] See Jer 4:31, in which the Lord predicts that His coming judgment would result in weakness comparable to labor pains.

[15] The phrase *chalah panim* occurs 16 times in 15 verses (Ex 32:11; 1 Sam 13:12; 1 Kgs 13:6 (twice); 2 Kgs 13:4; 2 Chr 33:12; Job 11:19; Ps 45:12; 119:58; Prov 19:6; Jer 26:19; Dan 13:12; Zech 7:2; 8:21–22; Mal 1:9) and conveys the idea of "entreaty." The phrase literally means "weaken the face of." When *chalah* (Hb. חָלָה) is used for entreaty, it occurs in the Piel stem. See also G. Seybold, "חָלָה *chalah*," in *TDOT*, ed. G. Johannes Botterweck and Helmer Ringgren; trans. David E. Green (Grand Rapids: Eerdmans, 1980): 4:407–9.

while others may have been ignorant. But the shepherd's responsibility to strengthen sheep is not contingent upon a sheep's awareness of his weakness.

The text does not indicate the cause of the weakness of the sheep. Some may have been weak because of circumstances, while for others the cause may have been sin. Perhaps some were physically weak while others were spiritually weak. Some could have been weakened from a lack of faith, and others from shallowness of faith. Some might have been weak as a result of their own actions, while others may have been suffering the consequences of the actions of others. But, regardless of why they were weak, the shepherd's responsibility was to help them to become strong.

That is the same for ministries in the church today. Shepherds will encounter sheep weakened by any number of circumstances. The responsibility to strengthen them is the same, but the manner by which they are strengthened will likely differ dramatically. As Gregory the Great observed nearly 1,500 years ago,[16] one does not minister to each the same. Different weaknesses require different kinds of strength administered by the shepherd. This verse is not a formula for how to strengthen weak sheep; it is a challenge to pursue the task.

In Scripture, Who Are the Weak?

There are multiple words conveying weakness used in many different contexts in Scripture. Physical weakness may be the result of natural causes like age (Ps 6:8), appearance (Gen 29:17), or lack of strength (Judg 16:7, 11, 16; 1 Pet 3:7). Or, it may be caused by external forces like fatigue (Exod 17:12), enemy attack (Ps 6:3), poverty (Exod 23:3; Acts 20:35), persecution (2 Cor 11:29–30), or oppression (Ps 12:5; Ezek 34:21). Words depicting weakness are also used at times to refer to the condition of supposed insignificance or the perception of lesser value than something else by comparison (1 Cor 1:27; 2:2–5; 4:10; 9:22; 12:22). Finally, the word

---

[16] See Gregory the Great, *Pastoral Care*, trans. Henry Davis (New York: Newman Press, 1950), 89–233. The entire third part of the book lists 36 different pairs of people to whom the pastor must be prepared to minister. The application is that pastors must minister to each personality type differently.

can refer to general human (fleshly) limitations (Rom 6:19; 8:3, 26; 1 Cor 15:43; 2 Cor 12:9; 13:3–4, 9; Heb 5:2; 7:18, 28).[17]

Types of Spiritual Weakness

Feeble Faith

Scripture cites several significant causes of spiritual weakness. First, some were feeble in faith. The Lord prayed for Peter, near the hour of the disciple's temptation, that his faith would not fail (Luke 22:32). However, knowing that Peter would weaken, Jesus further instructed him that once he was again strengthened in faith, he should strengthen others.[18]

Paul points to Abraham as an example of one who did not show weakness in faith: "And not being weaken in the faith, he . . . did not waver . . . through unbelief, but was strengthened in faith" (Rom 4:19–20). Instead, Abraham trusted in the Lord and in His plan. Thus, weakness of faith can cause people to doubt the Lord or His plan for their lives.

Paul also instructed the believers: "Receive one who is weak in the faith" (Rom 14:1), explaining that those "who are strong ought to bear with the scruples of the weak" (Rom 15:1). Those weak in faith were to be accepted into the fellowship but with limitations and support.[19]

---

[17] Augustine contends, "But of this we should have been wholly incapable, had not Wisdom condescended to adapt Himself to our weakness" (*On Christian Doctrine* 1.11, in *NPNF*[2], ed. Philip Schaff [Edinburgh: T&T Clark; Grand Rapids: Eerdmans, 1988], 525; http://www.ccel.org/ccel/schaff/npnf102.v.iv.xi.html).

[18] The Lord knew that Peter would fail but admonished him to strengthen others *after* he had returned. Like 2 Cor 1:3–4 where believers are encouraged to comfort others with the comfort by which they have been comforted, Peter was commanded to strengthen others with the strength by which he would be strengthened.

[19] Those weak in faith were not to be engaged with weighty arguments or disputes that might confuse them or discourage their faith (Rom 14:1). Moreover, they were also to be recognized and supported by those who were strong (Rom 15:1). Bob Deffinbaugh explains: "The difference between Paul's response to the weakness of Romans 14 and the heresy of Galatians can be best illustrated by his actions with regard to the circumcision of Timothy and Titus. In Acts 16:3, Paul had Timothy circumcised so as not to offend the scruples and custom (and perhaps prejudices) of those who knew that Timothy's father was a Greek. But in Gal 2:3–5, Paul refused to circumcise Titus because in that case the heretics were insisting that circumcision was essential to salvation" ("The Strong and the Weak (Romans 14)," from the series "Reasoning Through Romans," Bible.org, https://bible.org /seriespage/16-strong-and-weak-romans-14).

Furthermore, Paul admonished believers not to be "a stumbling block to those who are weak" in faith (1 Cor 8:9–12). He warned that inconsiderate believers could "wound . . . [the] weak conscience" of those with shallow faith, which could result in their eternal death. Paul called this carelessness of the strong, "sinning against Christ."

Thus, weakness of faith, as with Peter, could be an occasion for fear and disobedience, while the strengthening of faith could be an opportunity for testimony. Weakness of faith could cause one to miss God's plan for his life or to stumble over deep doctrines of the faith. It could even lead to eternal separation from God.

Immature Faith

A second kind of spiritual weakness that the Bible describes is an immaturity in faith. Jesus recognized this danger and cautioned the disciples to "watch and pray" because "the spirit indeed is willing, but the flesh is weak" (Matt 26:41). Similarly, Paul reminds his readers that the Holy Spirit "helps in our weaknesses" and intercedes for us before the Father (Rom 8:26).

This kind of weakness in maturity is also described in Heb 4:14–16. Here, the author points out that "we do not have a High Priest who cannot sympathize with our weaknesses." However, in verse 14, the believers are admonished, "[L]et us hold fast our confession," while verse 15 points out that Jesus did not give in to temptation. These verses suggest that the weakness referenced here pertains to those who have wavered in their confession or yielded to temptation.

At times, Scripture presents weakness stemming from immaturity as a lack of courage. This is often conveyed in the Hebrew text with a figurative expression combining various forms of the word *raphah* ("let drop"; *rapheh*, "weak, feeble, slack"; *riphyon*, "slackness") with the noun *yad* ("hand")—i.e., a weakening of the hand(s).[20] This phrase can denote those

---

[20] Cp. "forsake," Josh 10:6; "lost heart," 2 Sam 4:1; "weak," 17:2 and 2 Chr 15:7; "restrain your hand," 1 Chr 21:15 and 2 Chr 24:16; "discourage," Ezra 4:4; "hands will be weakened," Neh 6:9; "weak hands," Job 4:3 and Isa 35:3; "hands will be limp," Isa 13:7; "hands grow feeble," Jer 6:24; 50:43; "weakens the hands," Jer 38:4; "lacking courage," Jer 47:3; also see Ezek 7:17; 21:7; Zeph 3:16. See K. M. Beyse, "רָפָה," in *TDOT*, ed.

who are no longer vigilant and are consequently vulnerable (e.g., Isa 35:3; 2 Chr 15:7; Heb 12:12). A similar phrase relates to those who are weak in the knees.[21] Thus, when Paul admonished the believers in Corinth to "be brave, [and] be strong," he was appealing for courage. So, weakness in maturity of faith can cause believers to falter or yield to temptation when their faith is attacked or to lack the courage to stand when they are tested.

Weak or Absent Commitment

A third kind of spiritual weakness in Scripture relates to a weakness of character or the absence of a relationship with Christ.[22] This may be the case in 1 Thess 5:14 as Paul encouraged the believers to "help the weak." The believers regarded as "weak" may have been shrinking from persecution (1 Thess 3:3–5) or yielding to temptation (1 Thess 4:3–8).[23] The three groups described in this verse (unruly, faint, and weak) all seem to have a character deficiency related to them.

Debility of character is also apparent in Paul's use of *astheneō* in 1 Cor 8:7. The picture is of those who are outside of a relationship with God ("there is not in everyone that knowledge") and whose actions consequently demonstrate that they are "weak" and "defiled."[24] Similarly, Paul's reminder to the believers in Rom 5:6—"For when we were still without strength [*astheneō*] . . . Christ died for the ungodly"—points to a time when they were outside of a relationship with Christ. Thus, weakness can

---

G. Johannes Botterweck, Helmer Ringgren, and Heinz-Josef Fabry; trans. David E. Green (Grand Rapids: Eerdmans, 2004), 13:614-17. Scripture admonishes believers not to allow their hands to grow weak (2 Chr 15:7; Isa 35:3; Zeph 3:16; Heb 12:12). Jacob, in his blessing of Joseph, points out that Joseph's hands were made strong by the hands of the Lord (Gen 49:24).

[21] Job 4:4; Ps 109:24; Ezek 21:7; Isa 35:3. See also Martin Bucer, *Concerning the True Care of Souls*, trans. Peter Beale (Carlisle, PA: Banner of Truth Trust, 2013), 166–67.

[22] See Gustav Stählin, "ἀσθενής, ἀσθένεια, ἀσθενέω, † ἀσθένημα" in *TDNT*, ed. Gerhard Kittel and Gerhard Friedrich; trans. Geoffrey W. Bromiley (Grand Rapids: Eerdmans, 1964), 1:490-93. Stählin argues that this use of *astheneō* (ἀσθενέω) does not occur prior to the New Testament (492).

[23] Bucer, 165. See also Robert L. Thomas, *1 Thessalonians*, in *The Expositor's Bible Commentary*, ed. Frank E. Gæbelein (Grand Rapids: Zondervan, 1978), 11:289; and D. Michael Martin, *1, 2 Thessalonians*, NAC, vol. 33 (Nashville: B&H, 1995), 178.

[24] Mark Taylor, *1 Corinthians*, NAC, vol. 28 (Nashville: B&H, 2014), 207.

refer to actions that are inconsistent with the Christian life or indicative of those outside of a relationship with Him.

Disobedience

A final kind of spiritual weakness described in Scripture points to the effects of being under the judgment of God. In such cases, the corresponding weakness depicts the consequences of violating God's command. This weakness afflicted God's people corporately (Deut 29:22; Ps 107:5–6, 17) as well as individually (Ps 31:10; 1 Cor 11:30; Jas 5:14–16; cp. Mark 2:5). Thus, some weakness is a fallout from spiritual disobedience.

Many will remember the song from the children's television program *Sesame Street*, "Who are the people in your neighborhood?"[25] A more relevant question for shepherds is: Who are the weak among your flocks? It is imperative to know who they are if you are going to meet the expectation to strengthen them. Who are the weak in the context of your ministries? Scripture portrays the weak as those who are enfeebled physically or spiritually as a result of their circumstances or decisions. The kinds of weaknesses are many and the causes are manifold, but the Bible does not nuance our responsibility to strengthen the weak according to any particular cause of the weakness. Regardless of why their sheep are weak, shepherds are responsible for making them strong.

The Rod and the Staff: Strengthening the Weak

Merely identifying sheep as weak is not enough. In Ezekiel 34, God chastised the shepherds not for their ignorance but for their unresponsiveness. To be obedient to the responsibility entrusted to us as pastors, we must strive to make weak sheep strong. Fortunately, the Bible gives us part of the solution in order that we may know how to sustain the weary (Isa 50:4).

---

[25] Jeffrey Moss, "People in Your Neighborhood" (words and music), 1970.

Make the Weak Strong by Modeling Self-Discipline

One way to make the weak strong is by the example of your faith. Paul gave this admonition to the leaders in Ephesus (Acts 20:28–35): "Be on guard for yourselves and for all the flock" (Acts 20:28).[26] Such rigid self-examination was necessary because Paul knew that after he left, "savage wolves" would attack the flock to lure them away from the faith. The apostle knew that vigilance was necessary to "support the weak" (Acts 20:35). Thus, by hard work and self-discipline, the church leaders would help those who might be vulnerable to enemy attack.

Paul would later reiterate this message of self-discipline in the context of instructions regarding the Lord's Supper (1 Cor 11:28–31). He charged each believer to "examine himself" because many had become weak, sick, or worse as a consequence of their failure in self-discipline. So, by examining themselves, the believers would be a good example for others.[27] The pastor's vigilance, especially, sets a positive example—for the flock and even future generations—of the truth of God's love and the standards of His Word.[28]

Make the Weak Strong by Praying for Them

A second way to make the weak strong is through intercession. Believers have both an opportunity and an obligation to pray for the weak. This was James's instruction in Jas 5:13–16.[29] It was the responsibility of

---

[26] See also Richard Baxter, *The Reformed Pastor*, ed. William Brown (Carlisle, PA: The Banner of Truth Trust, 1999), 37–48. Baxter (1615–1691) originally designed this message as a challenge to a group of pastors in his association. He chose as his main text Acts 20:28 and admonished the the pastors to examine themselves first to be able to minister faithfully to others.

[27] See Taylor, *1 Corinthians*, 277–78. See also Heb 4:16. After talking about not giving in to temptation, the author admonishes us to pray for mercy and for grace—mercy for when we fail and grace to help us so that we do not fail.

[28] See Deut 29:10–22.

[29] Verse 14 asks, "Is anyone among you sick [Gk. *asthenei*, lit. "be weak, without strength"]?" The verb *astheneō* certainly can mean "is sick" in this context and is generally translated that way. However, as seen earlier in this chapter, the word can have significance broader than just sickness. Note the last phrase in verse 15, "If he has committed sins, he will be forgiven." James 5:15 indicates that the prayer of the righteous "will save (Gk. *sōsei*) the sick" (Gk. *kamnonta*, "one who is sick"). Here, James uses a different word than in 5:14 to describe those being "saved." The verb *kamnō* can mean "be weary or sick." It

the leaders to intercede for the *asthenei* (Gk., "one who is sick").[30] Similarly, Paul prayed that the believers in Corinth would be strong even if he was weak (2 Cor 13:9).[31]

Believers have a responsibility to pray for those in need. They pray for God's healing and for His strength. As shepherds, prayer is our strongest weapon. In prayer we bring the needs of the sheep before the true Shepherd, and in preaching we present the true Shepherd to the sheep in their need. We need to be reminded of and challenged by the words of Samuel, who promised the people, "Far be it from me that I should sin against the LORD in ceasing to pray for you" (1 Sam 12:23).

Make the Weak Strong by Caring for Them

A third way that shepherds can strengthen sheep is by caring for those who cannot care for themselves. James described this as "pure and undefiled religion" (Jas 1:27).[32] This also seems to be the point of Paul's instruction in Acts 20:35. There, Paul related to the early church leaders the moral obligation of caring for those who could not care for themselves.[33] Paul described his personal practice of hard work and commended that same practice to other leaders so they might be able to "support the weak."

In a world where seeing people ask for money on the side of the road is a common occurrence, to become cynical or jaded to the real needs of people is easy. If we err, it should be on the side of compassion. We must never allow those who pretend to have needs to prevent us from attending to those who are genuinely in need.

---

occurs in only one other place in the New Testament—Heb 12:3, "become weary." The word is used twice in the LXX (Job 10:1 and 17:2) and conveys the idea of weariness in both. Perhaps those being "saved" by the prayers of the righteous include those who were weary and not just those who were physically sick.

[30] See also Pss 31:9–10 and 107:5–6, in which the psalmist prays for himself in his weakness.

[31] Cp. Matt 26:41; Mark 14:38; Rom 8:25–27.

[32] See Matt 25:31–46, especially vv. 40 and 45. See also Amos 2:6 and Mal 3:5. Amos declared that one of the reasons God cited for His judgment on Israel was their abuse of the poor; Malachi announced God's judgment on those who oppress His people.

[33] Darrell L. Bock, *Acts*, BECNT (Grand Rapids: Baker Academic, 2007), 632. See also John B. Polhill, *Acts*, NAC, vol. 26 (Nashville: B&H, 1992), 429.

Make the Weak Strong by Identifying with Their Weaknesses

A fourth way that shepherds can strengthen weak sheep is by identifying with the weaknesses of people in order to minister to them. This was Paul's testimony in 1 Cor 9:22 when he determined to become weak in order to minister to those who were in that same condition. The immediate context of this passage describes both Jews (v. 20) and Gentiles (v. 21) who were outside of a relationship with Christ. Paul's passion was to win them to Christ. The reference to the weak in verse 22 seems to function as a summative reference to all (Jews or Gentiles) who were without Christ.[34] Paul's becoming weak refers to his choice to give up some of his personal liberties in order to minister to them more effectively.[35]

The ultimate example here is Christ, who "emptied himself" (Phil 2:7, CSB) and became as one of us to point us to the Father. We must never allow the world of selfie sticks and personal pronouns (YouTube, Myspace, iTunes, iPad, iPhone) to cloud our responsibility to care for others, lest we find ourselves narcissistically taking pictures of ourselves while the world languishes. Pastoral care is a recapturing of the second person singular and the third person plural pronouns. We must see beyond ourselves to strengthen them.

Make the Weak Strong by Upholding Them

A fifth way that we can strengthen the weak among our flocks is by holding them up. This is Paul's charge to the Thessalonians (1 Thess 5:14). Upholding the weak could convey the idea of ministering to those caught in moral weakness.[36] Another way for you to uphold the weak is by holding up their arms as in the case of Aaron and Hur (Exod 17:12). Finally, the

---

[34] Taylor, 220–21. Taylor notes that the verb tense here is perfect as opposed to aorist to indicate a "settled conviction/manner of life that Paul had taken up for the cause of winning the most people possible to Christ."

[35] Cp. 1 Cor 8:13, "[I]f food makes my brother stumble, I will never again eat meat."

[36] See footnote 23 above.

idea of helping the weak in 1 Thess 5:14 can also carry the idea of showing concern for[37] or even holding before your face.[38]

In any case, the idea of helping the weak by holding them up implies the proactive concern of the strong. Whatever the infirmity of the weak, the responsibility of the strong is to hold them up.

Make the Weak Strong by Genuine Acceptance but Prudent Exposure

Paul's point regarding the weak in Rom 14:1 is vital to the effective maturation of believers and reveals a sixth way to strengthen the weak. In the context of discussing matters of spiritual maturity, he advocates genuine reception of the weak into the body but advises caution in exposing them to matters reserved for the mature. Thus, you can help make the weak strong by allowing their involvement in the body to be appropriate to their level of spiritual development. This action has nothing to do with special knowledge or degrees of importance in the body. But, it has everything to do with allowing less mature believers to grow in the faith at a healthy rate without prematurely exposing them to matters that they lack the spiritual depth to appropriate.

Candidly, many churches fail in this matter in relation to pastor search committees. Serving on such committees allows less mature members often to be exposed to more delicate church-related matters and to become overwhelmed and often disillusioned. We must show discernment in working with the weak and helping them to grow healthily to maturity.

Make the Weak Strong by Encouraging Those Who Lack Courage

A seventh way the strong can help the weak is through encouragement. Isaiah gives this instruction regarding those who may be lacking

---

[37] Hermann Hanse, "ἔχω," in *TDNT*, ed. Gerhard Kittel and Gerhard Friedrich, trans. Geoffrey W. Bromiley (Grand Rapids: Eerdmans, 1964), 2:816–32.

[38] See Gary W. Demarest, *1, 2 Thessalonians, 1, 2 Timothy, Titus*, The Communicator's Commentary (Waco: Word Books, 1984), 93–94. Demarest sees this as a word picture describing the need for the strong to mentor the weak by paying close attention to them and "keeping oneself face to face with someone."

in hope (Isa 35:3–4). He challenges them to strengthen the hands of the weak, reminding them that the Messiah is coming and He will save. In a related context, Zephaniah encourages Judah to be strong (Zeph 3:16), remembering that the Lord is "in your midst" and He "will save" (3:17). Similarly, the writer of Hebrews calls believers to courage and strength in the face of the Lord's discipline. He wants the believers to know that the Lord loves them (Heb 13:6) and is calling them to life (13:9) and holiness (13:10). Even so, we can encourage those who are weak by reminding them that God is strong, by showing them why we have reasons to trust Him, and by championing the hope of His ultimate return.

Make the Weak Strong by Pointing Them to Jesus

Ultimately, the greatest help that the strong can give the weak is to point them to Jesus. He is the good Shepherd (Ezek 34:23), and He is the only One who can truly make them strong (34:16).[39] As Thielicke explains, "Jesus Christ did not remain at the base headquarters in heaven, receiving reports of the world's suffering from below and shouting a few encouraging words from a safe distance."[40] Christ came to save weak sheep. He is the One who is strong when we are weak (2 Cor 12:10); who became weak for us (1 Cor 15:43; 2 Cor 8:9); who sympathizes with our weaknesses (Heb 4:15–16); who pleads the cause of the weak (Prov 22:22–23); who ministers to us in our weakness (2 Cor 13:1–5); and who strengthens the weak (Ezek 34:16). There may be more that we can do after we have pointed weak sheep to Jesus; but until we do, nothing else matters.

---

[39] Cp. Ezek 34:4 and 34:16. In v. 16, *chalah* (חָלָה) should probably be rendered "weak." In v. 4, we know that the first use of *chalah* means "weak" because of the divine instructions to make them strong *chazaq* (חָזַק), as virtually every English translation renders it. Oddly (and inconsistently) many of those same versions inexplicably render *chalah* as "sick" in v. 16, despite the same use of *chazaq* (חָזַק) as in verse 4. For consistency, had the author intended for this word to be rendered "sick," he most likely would have used *rapha'* (רָפָא) to emphasize the Lord's healing as he did in verse 4 to depict His instructions to the shepherds. See Isa 39:1 for a similar use of *chalah* and *chazaq*. See also Carl Philip Weber, "חָלָה," in *TWOT*, 1:286. Weber argues that in Ezek 34:16, "No distinction need be made between 'sick' or 'weak,' the latter resulting from the former." His argument may have merit, but for consistency, *chalah* should be rendered "weak" in 34:16.

[40] Helmut Thielicke, *Christ and the Meaning of Life* (New York: Harper & Row, 1962), 18.

The country of Wales was the site of one of the greatest revivals in the history of Christianity. In 1904, Evan Roberts was a 26-year-old miner and blacksmith with no real theological training, but he had a heart to see God work. He prayed fervently that God would bend him, and God used him in a mighty way.

He began to preach a simple message:

1. Confess all known sin to God, receiving forgiveness through Jesus Christ.
2. Remove anything from your life that you are in doubt of or feel unsure about.
3. Be totally yielded and obedient to the Holy Spirit.
4. Publicly confess the Lord Jesus Christ.

In 1904–1905, an estimated 100,000 people out of a total population of 1.5 million came to faith in Jesus Christ in just six months. At the height of the revival, crime rates plummeted, bars and jails were emptied, and churches were full.[41]

Today, if you go to Wales, the scene is much different. I learned recently about an organization within the Church of Wales that exists to sell church buildings that no longer serve as places of worship.

My interest began when a book I was reading referenced a For Sale sign in front of a church in Wales. Curious, I did an internet search on "churches for sale in Wales," thinking I would find a picture of a church building with a For Sale sign as the book described.

What I discovered is an organization called Redundant Churches. It exists to sell the property of churches after they close their doors. The website reveals buildings across the country that were once alive, vibrant churches but that now mark the landscape as empty tombs—relics of a past many no longer remember.[42]

In addition to the sadness of so many churches closing their doors, the name struck me as curious—"redundant" churches. It suggests saturation,

---

[41] J. Edwin Orr, *Flaming Tongue: The Impact of 20th Century Revivals* (Chicago: Moody Press, 1973), 15.

[42] See http://www.churchinwales.org.uk/structure/representative-body/property /redundant-churches-2/; accessed January 16, 2017.

overpopulation, and the message, "We've got all the churches that we need. Any more churches would be simply redundant." What a sad picture of a denomination that has lost its vision and impact and is now losing its facilities!

The tragedy is even more poignant when you consider the sheep suffering under an increasingly enfeebled church. Were the shepherds redundant as well? Or, had they become so distracted feeding themselves that they did not notice the weakening sheep?

There may be many reasons for the weakening of the churches in Wales. But one thing is clear: What once was strong somehow became weak. Not enough faithful shepherds were there to make it strong again.

That is precisely the picture God is highlighting in Ezekiel 34—a weakening flock and inadequate shepherds. We must awaken to the unacceptable numbers of feeble sheep within our flocks and own our responsibility to make them strong again.

CHAPTER 4

Healing: The Forgotten Art of the Church

Paige Patterson

T he healing ministry of the church is both vigorously embraced and
passionately rejected in the contemporary malaise. When a loved one
is assaulted by debilitating illness, the church is rushed to the prayer rails
of intercession but with little hope of cure and almost no grasp of what
may be expected of God in this crisis. The presence of charlatans offering
healing, often for an investment of capital in their ministries, together with
the sad spectacle of broken hearts and lives when healing is denied, has
exacerbated the issue to the point that many churches react to the exploitation of the sheep by leaning so far away from the responsibility of meeting
human needs that little hope is offered for those who suffer.

Is there a theology of healing and suffering in the Bible? Is "healing" in the atonement of Christ? Does the church have a responsibility
beyond perfunctory prayer? Is there a link between the healing ministries
of the church and the task of reaching the people of the world for Christ?
What promises can the church legitimately make to sufferers? These are
the kinds of questions that congregations need to answer and pastors need
to address.

According to Ezekiel 34, the irresponsible shepherd is excoriated for
failure to have strengthened the weak: "nor have you healed those who

were sick" (v. 4). On the other hand, God promises that as the good Shepherd, He Himself will "strengthen what was sick" (v. 16). Admittedly, contemporary shepherds cannot match the abilities and actions of the great Shepherd of our souls. But certainly, the church should hear the challenge of Ezekiel to be the shepherds of the sheep modeled after the good Shepherd and not after the failed example of the irresponsible shepherds who face the judgment of God.

The Causes of Illness

The journey to an encounter with the God of wellness must begin with an etiology of illness. Why do people become ill? Are they at fault for these physical maladies? First, acknowledgment must be made that all illness and suffering is related to sin. Insofar as the biblical record is concerned, there was no death for our parents in the garden of Eden. There was a threat of death as the penalty for eating of "the tree of the knowledge of good and evil" (Gen 2:17). But there is no certain indication that Adam had ever seen death of any kind, though some theologians and scientists suggest that animal death had occurred. The absence of death presupposes that sickness and suffering were also absent from the utopian conditions of splendor in that paradise.

The encounter of the first humans with the tempter led to a failure in gratitude through the deceit of the serpent. Everything was in the possession of Adam except for one tree. Rather than delighting in the generosity of God, they coveted that which He forbade. The penalty was exacted—death, which was immediate in its spiritual dimension and began immediately in its physical dimension to be played out painfully in sickness and sorrow until physical death ended the journey on earth. This horror would even manifest itself in the agony of producing new life (Gen 3:16). In this sense, all suffering and sickness has its origin in man's rebellion against his greatest benefactor.

By the same token, some sickness, though not all sickness, is the direct product of sinful behavior. Paul confronted the Corinthian church with the fact that because some came to the Lord's Table in an unworthy manner, some became ill and some had even died (1 Cor 11:27–30). Were the contemporary churches to take that seriously, the celebration of the Lord's Supper would assume new meaning, to say the least. But the point is that a wrong approach to the Table of the Lord was the cause of illness.

Every death shouts the impact of sin, and this is especially true of the hideous impact of war, in which even the innocent are inevitably visited with the consequences of human covetousness. Even those who believe, as I do, that in a fallen world a just war may be necessary must confess that sin is the cause of every war. Those suffering from lung cancer frequently have to know that they brought on the disease by smoking. AIDS victims have often induced the onset of illness by drug use or homosexual liaisons. In fact, all venereal disease is the direct result of sinful rebellion against God's plan and purpose. Astonishingly, venereal diseases of all varieties constitute the most easily eliminated epidemic faced by the human family. If sexual intimacy were practiced as God prescribed—one man for one woman for life—such maladies would vanish in two generations. Many diseases such as diabetes are not infrequently caused by lack of fitness in lifestyle and discipline.

Purposes for Illness and Suffering

There are other purposes for illness and suffering. One that seems strange but should not surprise us is that God often uses suffering evangelistically. When Paul was shipwrecked on Malta, he was bitten by a venomous serpent. At first the natives concluded that Paul was a murderer. But when no harm came to him, "they changed their minds and said that he was a god" (Acts 28:1–10). Or again, after suffering the flogging and imprisonment in Philippi, God used that suffering to bring about the conversion of the jailor and his family (Acts 16:22–34). All of this is to say nothing of the suffering of Christ on the cross and the global impact of that suffering.

Other illness is didactic in nature. It teaches the sufferer, or others, lessons that often cannot be grasped in other ways. Out of his suffering, Job learned the greatness of God (Job 40:3–5). Paul confessed that from his "thorn in the flesh" he learned the adequacy of God's grace (2 Cor 12:7–10). Joseph, in Canaan and in Egypt, was introduced to God's purposes in tribulation, working out the saving of his entire family (Gen 45:7–8). Hosea experienced the heartache of an unfaithful wife in order to preach to Israel effectively about their unfaithfulness to Yahweh (Hos 3).

Given the fact that all the godly shall suffer (2 Tim 3:12), what should be the response of the believer to illness and suffering? First, a believer should subject his life and heart to the evaluation of the Holy Spirit. Is there known or unknown iniquity in one's life that has caused this sorrow? As nearly as can be determined, if there seems to be no sinful cause for the illness, then the Christian will do well to search for the evangelistic opportunity that looms before him. Years ago, Tori Soritau, a little girl about four years of age, was diagnosed in Romania with incurable cancer. Physicians in Fort Worth confirmed the diagnosis but launched treatment anyway. Tori is now prospering, but few know how many physicians, nurses, and other folks associated with her care eventually came to Christ. I do not suggest that God afflicted this child, but beyond all doubt, God used her suffering to bring many to Christ.[1]

Perhaps the Lord of all the earth is teaching. Our adversities are almost always God's universities. I would reluctantly have to admit that I have learned more about God and His grace through my sorrows than through whatever victories I have celebrated. Discovering the power of God in the crucible of suffering is the testimony of most great men and women of faith.

Having been assured by an obstetrician that my daughter Carmen, though underweight, was fine, I turned to comfort my wife, who was recovering from a caesarian section. Somehow I knew the information from the doctor was incorrect. Within an hour, Carmen's life was in grave jeopardy. When the sedative had taken effect and my wife slept, I found my way to the small chapel in the Baptist hospital in New Orleans. Alone with God and an open Bible, there played out a titanic clash of wills— God's versus my own. There I finally learned to trust God and bend to His will. Carmen miraculously survived and today is a wonderful pastor's wife and the mother of my two grandchildren, but I am convinced that what I

---

[1] See Tori's own book recounting this amazing story of God's grace, written with the assistance of her parents: Raelene and Ilie Soriţău: *A Princess Story: A Story of Hope, Faith, and Miracles* (Oradea, RO: Editura *Universităţii* Emanuel, 2011).

learned about God that night was critical to all future ministry in more ways than I can easily count.

Finally, there is illness that remains always inexplicable. Job had no idea for an extensive period why he was suffering and probably never understood the cosmic confrontation in which he was an unwilling player. But while he never understood, he did learn about God; and he learned to trust God. His affirmations of faith remain remarkable.

Is Healing in the Atonement?

In 1934, William Edward Biederwolf penned a powerful answer to this question entitled *Whipping-Post Theology*, in which he strongly argued that healing of the body was not on the docket of the New Testament.[2] While I agree with the concern that Biederwolf addressed and while clearly the major issue in the atonement is the healing of the soul, I do believe that this Presbyterian evangelist overlooked the obvious. If it is true that all sickness and suffering is the result of the Fall, then it is also true that the saving of the atonement touches everything forfeited in the Fall. The glorified body itself is the product of redemption and hence owes its origin to the cross of Christ. In that sense healing is certainly in the atonement. Jesus wore a crown of thorns depicting clearly God's intention through the atonement to heal the impact of sin's curse on the earth.

All temporal healing, however, can scarcely be a part of the atonement for two reasons. First, the healing is temporal in nature. Humans become ill again and, in fact, ultimately die. The healing of the atonement is eternal. When that healing occurs, the recipient lives forever without illness or pain. The former things have passed away. This takes nothing away from the fact that God sometimes miraculously heals. However, the emphasis remains where it ought to be, namely, on the supernatural healing of both soul and body never to be undone.

Second, God does not always elect to heal temporal bodies. Sometimes, as in the case of Paul, God simply responds that His grace is sufficient (2 Cor 12:9). Yet, one can be sure that Paul in his glorified body will

---

[2] William Edward Biederwolf, *Whipping-Post Theology, or Did Jesus Atone for Disease?* (Grand Rapids: Eerdmans, 1934).

not carry the thorn in his flesh. By the same token, there is no indication that anyone coming to Christ for the salvation of his soul is ever denied. To the contrary, the Scriptures assert that those who come to Him will never be denied (John 6:37).

Scripture abounds with cases of healing denied. Already, we have focused on Paul, the missionary-theologian of the earliest church. Three times he sought deliverance from the thorn in the flesh and was consistently denied (2 Cor 12:8–9). Paul left Trophimus, who was sick, in Miletus (2 Tim 4:20). Why not heal the man rather than leaving him to suffer? If healing is in that sense in the atonement and Paul had the gifts of healing, why not practice this gift with Trophimus? In the favorite verse of every backsliding evangelical, Paul tells Timothy not to imbibe water any further but to drink a little wine (1 Tim 5:23). Why risk making an alcoholic of his son in the ministry? Heal his stomach disorder! And what do we make of the unfortunate Jacob, who had a late night meeting with the angel of the Lord and was permanently wounded so that he hobbled the remainder of his life (Gen 32:22–32)? One might rather expect to have a meeting with God and be healed. And why is it that even healing evangelists die, as do we all?

The nature of healing in the Bible is also decisively shocking in contrast to modern "miraculous healings." The dead are raised to life, the blind are made to see, an amputated ear is restored to a man's head, leprosy is cured and verified by a priest, an issue of blood is staunched, a withered hand is restored to vigorous activity, and a paralytic is not only forgiven of his sin but sent home carrying his bed with him. All of these healings were rather dramatic, did not involve the interchange of money from the poor to the prosperous evangelist, and all were public and obvious, to the astonishment of observers.

Occasionally one hears about someone being raised to life from the dead. I, for one, have no issue with such reports as far as it concerns the ability of God to effect such. But the strange aspect is that these seemingly always turn out to be difficult to verify, staged in a remote area, and not subject to any sort of known verification. On the other hand, the biblical miracles of healing were seldom private affairs and were always open to the inspection of the critic. Take the resurrection of Lazarus as a case in point. Left deliberately for three days, as if to prove that he was really dead, he was called forth and needed assistance from astonished onlookers with being unwrapped and loosed (John 11:44). This is all in sharp contrast to the claims often featured today.

The Rod and the Staff: Healing Ministry

Acts 28:8–9 provides a snapshot of the healing ministry of the early church. Wrecked on the island of Malta, Paul found that the father of the leading citizen, Publius, was sick with a fever and dysentery. Paul prayed for him, and the man was healed (Gk. *iaomai*). Then others on the island came and were also healed (Gk. *therapeuō*). This may be a simple literary change of word that means the same thing. More probably, the last word suggests the practice of medicine whereas the former suggests divine intervention. Whether or not this is a proper conclusion, it does suggest the appropriate work of the church in any era. Practicing medicine and divine intervention are both in the realm of church practice.

Gifts of healings are promised to the church. Although cessationists believe that the sign gifts ceased with the writing of the New Testament, such a conclusion cannot be proven. What is important to comprehend is that these gifts of healings are vitally connected to the prayer life of the church. A critical passage for this understanding is James 5:13–18.

According to this text, anyone suffering is to avail himself of the power of prayer. He is to remain as cheerful as possible, singing psalms. Then, if he wishes, he may call for the elders of the church who will pray over him, anointing him with oil. Spiros Zodhiates, in his superb treatment of the book of James, argues that this practice was primarily therapeutic.[3] I do not find his argument convincing, and I prefer to understand the anointing of oil to be symbolic. For several reasons, clearly the anointing oil as such is not involved in the healing process. First, this text is the only one of many on healing where such a practice is suggested. Second, the text plainly states that the prayer of faith saves the sick. Why then anoint with oil?

---

[3] Spiros Zodhiates, *The Patience of Hope: The Epistle of James and the Life of Faith, An Exposition of James 4:13–5:20* (Grand Rapids: Eerdmans, 1960), 125–27.

The use of anointing oil in healing functions is like baptism in the salvation experience. Baptism does not save the penitent. He is saved as a result of godly sorrow that produces repentance unto salvation (2 Cor 7:10). But baptism is a public profession of his faith that perfectly pictures his death to the old life and his resurrection to newness of life. Oil is one of the symbols of the Holy Spirit (1 John 2:20). The prayer of faith saves the sick, but the anointing of oil is a public reference to the active agency of the Holy Spirit in the healing process.

When the elders gather to pray for the sick, they may anoint with oil as a symbol of the intervention of the Holy Spirit. However, the use of a small bottle of oil held between the thumb and third finger, turned upside down to produce a drop of the liquid, which, in turn, is slapped to the head of the sick, is a poor substitute for anointing biblically. Psalm 133:2 presents the reader with an example of biblical anointing. Aaron is anointed as priest from a horn of oil. When this is poured lavishly over his head, the oil courses down the beard and onto the edges of his garments. This is a portrait of the giving of the Holy Spirit without measure. The prolific dose of oil suggests the abundance of the availability of the Spirit for this healing ministry.

Prayer

How then shall the church respond to the challenge of physical malady? There are four distinct roles for the church in the ministry of healing. First, prayer for the sick is always in order. Consequently, such prayer should be encouraged as a part of every service of worship. The problem is not that this often occurs. The problem is that prayer for physical healing predominates over intercessory prayer on behalf of the lost. More time should be devoted to petitioning God to heal the souls of those in need of salvation than to prayer for the healing of the body, which, in any event, is temporary. Nevertheless, the heartfelt, specific prayer for the healing of the Lord is always appropriate. Such intercession should include not merely a plea for healing but also prayer for spiritual growth and for usefulness through the suffering.

This prayer should frequently be made a part of the pastoral prayer. The shepherd of the flock, concerned for his sheep, will offer intercession to God for the health of his sheep. This ought to be done both publicly and privately.

Public Invitation

A second approach to pastoral healing concerns the use of the public invitation. As a sermon concludes, exhortation is often a part of that message. This approach has usually driven those hearing the invitation to respond to the claims of Christ in a variety of ways, but most importantly to confess Christ and receive Him as Savior. What if a pastor were to include in his exhortation the offer to pray for those who had need of healing? And make the diaconate available to assist the pastor and pray for those in need of healing or who have friends or relatives in need of prayer? One pastor who had this practice noted a sharp rise in the number of lost people visiting his church each Sunday. Further, many who came forward for prayer, when counseled by thoughtful and well-prepared deacons, proceeded to make decisions to receive Christ as Savior. The invitation became more participatory and meaningful, and the number of people coming to Christ increased. People facing problems also began to respond, seeking intercession on their behalf by the deacons.

Observing this, I began preaching on the subject of healing and soliciting the assistance of deacons during the invitation. The response has been beyond all that I could have anticipated. People believe that God cares for their lives and souls. They believe that He has promised to hear and answer prayer. As a result, when given the opportunity, they respond to this call and present themselves for prayer. Accordingly, the number of people coming to Christ also increased. Deacons find fresh meaning in service to the congregation through earnest prayer.

Pastoral Visitation

A third approach reverts to the role of pastoral visitation in hospitals, homes for the elderly, etc. This element of the shepherd's task, as often as not, is delegated to subordinates. Yet there are few means that lead to attaining closeness to the congregation and ministering to the needs of the flock like such visitation. Here, too, is the most obvious place for the anointing of oil if that is requested. Such visits do not require an inordinate expenditure of time with each patient. But the sheep deserve the attention and prayer of the shepherd.

Pastoral Counseling

Given the fact that there is much to be learned in times of illness, the fourth arena for pastoral ministry encompasses the area of counsel. Pastoral counseling far surpasses all other venues for counsel in the dark hours of illness, sorrow, and heartache. Finding comfort in carefully selected readings from God's Word, discovering the multiplied facets of God's grace and fresh vistas of His greatness, offers to the pastor a teaching ministry that is often not available through preaching alone. Assisting the sufferer to find meaning and significance in the hour of trial for the kind-hearted shepherd is a ministry that knows no bounds.

Conclusion

The path for healing in the contemporary church begins with the communication to the flock that God does not always choose to heal. He may respond affirmatively and heal immediately. He may elect to grant special extension of His grace for bearing a disease with confidence in the providence of God. Or God may respond, "No healing at present but at a later time." However, *it is never wrong to ask God to intervene and heal.* It is always right to come to the throne of grace in time of need.

The benefits of appearing before God in prayer are profound even when healing is not granted. Comfort arises when a person comes into God's presence. Endurance in the difficulties of life is gained from kneeling before the God of the universe. The fellowship of prayer is valuable to the whole congregation. Understanding the will and purposes of God often is clarified when the one suffering illness appears before the Lord.

The reinstitution of meaningful healing ministry in the church is in order. Insufficient is the reaction against the abuses on television and elsewhere, which leads to the failure to minister and pray. As Ezekiel points out, the great Shepherd will care for the flock and the undershepherd comes under the judgment of God when he does not meet the needs of his sheep.

Not all ministries of the pastor are of equal importance. The preaching of God's Word and the evangelization of the lost are certainly more important than the ministry of healing, but the neglect of the healing ministry can only establish guilt and judgment.

CHAPTER 5

Shepherds Must Bind Up the Broken

Dale Johnson

B rokenness is all too familiar in the human experience because the curse of the world has made it common. Sometimes life seems to ebb and flow from one disappointment to another. Many of our recollections seem to have their orbit around life's distresses. So acquainted are we with brokenness that it is more like describing the intimate memories of a dear old friend than trying to recall the name of a man you once met. Brokenness is not an abstract thought you try to wrap your mind around—not like hearing of a faraway place to which you have never been, but something known intimately through personal experience.

As a broad category, to be broken is not limited to the physical essence of being. Brokenness rightly includes internal vexation and could be described as an exposure of the soul. The soul veiled in flesh is comfortable, not realizing its own self-destruction. Content with imminent pleasures that mask a slow deterioration, the soul seeking lesser comforts is left dry and thirsty. The soul hidden in Christ is at peace and secure. When the believer experiences storms and heartache, the hope of Christ's coming to make all things new protects the soul from complete despair. In contrast, the soul that has been unveiled, without finding hope in the Sovereign, is broken. The exposed soul aches for comfort, satisfaction, and peace.

Pain and suffering are real in this broken world, and we must not pretend otherwise. As believers, we do not have to fear pain or let our hearts be troubled in this present darkness. Our brokenness is a reminder that we are human and not divine. Even though our hearts and flesh fail, "God is the strength of my heart and my portion forever" (Ps 73:26). Shepherds are to lead the broken, rebellious, tired, weary, and weak to Christ to find rest for their souls. This chapter aims to demonstrate that the task of shepherding includes active personal participation in leading the broken to Christ, the only balm that restores the soul. We want our people to see Christ, to know Him, to understand their hurts and fears from His perspective; and we must guide them to that refuge and rock. Broken people have the opportunity to experience Christ in a way that destroys abstract belief about Him so that they may be as confident as Job in their declaration, "I had heard rumors about You, but now my eyes have seen You" (Job 42:5, NASB).

The duty to feed the sheep and bind the broken ultimately rests in the hands of God. As Stephen Rummage will explain in chapter 10, the duty neglected by earthly shepherds will be finally completed by the true Shepherd. In Ezek 34:16, God promises to fulfill the duty neglected by earthly shepherds. God will judge the shepherds for their derelict deeds. The shepherd's task is to represent accurately the character of the living God to His people. Pastoral responsibility to bind the broken reflects the character of the good Shepherd and aids the people with appropriate application of the truths of God's written Word.

The intimate work of binding the broken involves dressing the seeping wounds of the soul. Nearness is necessary to bind wounds, but that nearness is often unsanitary. Christ, the good Shepherd, demonstrated that binding the broken was hands-on work. He came to the earth to dwell among us, to taste our suffering and weakness, and to endure the brunt of our fall into death.[1] He compassionately touched the wounded and broken in spirit as One who identified with them, not as one who feared dirty hands.[2]

---

[1] John 1:14; Heb 2:14–18; Heb 5:2.
[2] Matt 8:3; 9:29–30; Mark 5:22–42.

Binding the Broken

Consider the statement of the Lord in Ezek 34:4, spoken by the prophet, "[Y]ou have not . . . bound up the broken." The shepherds of Israel neglected a duty for which God would hold them accountable. Through the prophet, God gave a warning of "Woe" and proclamation "against" the shepherds. They were supposed to feed the sheep with the words of God—a lesson learned by Israel in the wilderness: "Man shall not live by bread alone; but man lives by every word that proceeds from the mouth of the LORD" (Deut 8:3). The shepherds' negligence left unbound the broken among the sheep.

In order to clarify God's expectations for the shepherd, pastors must arrive at a clear understanding of the phrase "bind up the broken" (Ezek 34:16). In this case, to "be broken" (Hb. *shavar*) refers to those who have been broken into pieces.[3] This brokenness can be viewed in reference to physical and inner frailty. Ezekiel does not limit brokenness to inward vexation of the soul, though that seems to be the thrust in this passage. The same word is used in Ezek 6:9 to describe the pain God felt at Israel's rebellion: "I was crushed by their adulterous heart which has departed from Me, and by their eyes which play the harlot after their idols."

The Broken: Sheep without a Shepherd

The essence of God's character as the good Shepherd does not depend on the proper representation of earthly shepherds. However, the sheep's view of God may be altered by the shepherd's misrepresentation of Him. This was one reason Jesus was displeased with the Pharisees and Sadducees. These "religious leaders" claimed to know God and speak for Him, but they misrepresented His true character. The same can be said for the shepherds in Ezekiel 34. The shepherds did not accurately represent the character of the good Shepherd. Thus, the people were, in one sense, "sheep having no shepherd" (Matt 9:36; Mark 6:34). Moreover, with the absence of a shepherd, the people inevitably begin to wander.

---

[3] Victor P. Hamilton, "שָׁבַר, שָׁבוּר," in *TWOT*, 2:901–2.

Israel's wandering resulted from their refusal to hear God's Word (see Ezek 14). The people rebelled against the ordinances of the Lord and did not walk according to His statutes (Ezek 5:5–8). Their hearts were damaged, and the people sought to assuage the inner hurt with detestable idols in the sanctuary of God (5:11). Moreover, the shepherds had led the sheep toward idols by their own practice (14:1–8). Ezekiel explained that the idols had become a stumbling block that hindered their hearts from knowing God. God declared that the shepherds would bear the punishment of their sin in order "that the house of Israel may no longer stray from Me, nor be profaned any more with all their transgressions" (14:11). The idols blurred the vision of the people so that they could not see God. Their estranged hearts led to multiplied brokenness. By God's design, people who are without His Word are broken people.

Current Binding Methods

God designed shepherds to be physicians of the soul. However, recent trends have led to an abandonment of the traditional understanding of pastoral care.[4] Andrew Purves argues that the classical tradition of pastoral care was "much more constrained by matters of theology."[5] Theological categories of pain and suffering were replaced with psychological categories of human experience. However, the way we choose to categorize wounds of the soul inevitably dictates our categories for treatment. Therapeutics in pastoral care came to revolve around an anthropology undergirded by humanistic psychology and "symbolic interpretations of God."[6]

---

[4] See Thomas Oden, *Care of Souls in the Classic Tradition* (Philadelphia: Fortress, 1984). The following authors demonstrate that classic pastoral care was abandoned in favor of Seward Hiltner's new pastoral theology (*Preface to Pastoral Theology: The Ministry and Theory of Shepherding* [Nashville: Abingdon Press, 1958]): Andrew Purves, *Pastoral Theology in the Classical Tradition* (Louisville: Westminster John Knox, 2001); Charles Kemp, *Physicians of the Soul: A History of Pastoral Counseling* (New York: The Macmillan Company, 1947); Leroy Aden and J. Harold Ellens, eds., *Turning Points in Pastoral Care: The Legacy of Anton Boisen and Seward Hiltner* (Grand Rapids: Baker, 1990); Philip Rieff, *The Triumph of the Therapeutic: Uses of Faith After Freud* (Wilmington, DE: ISI Books, 2006).

[5] Purves, *Pastoral Theology in the Classical Tradition*, 3.

[6] Ibid., 3.

Jeremiah warned the shepherds of Judah against this very trend. He rebuked the shepherds for trying to assuage the broken hearts of Israel "slightly" (Jer 6:14; 8:11; cp. "superficially," CSB). Everyone was greedy for selfish gain. The wicked prophets misled the people by speaking "visions from their own minds" and not words "from the LORD's mouth" (Jer 23:16–17). The futility led the flock of God to a wilderness of fleeting peace, rather than green pastures and quiet waters. The same message from the two prophets could be used as a warning today. Many current methods of pastoral care have been compromised by systems that lend themselves to selfish ambitions and superficial remedies.

Selfish Ambition

Professionalism and secular psychology, like a two-horned bull, threaten the call of the shepherd to bind the broken. Shepherds embracing the CEO model of pastoral ministry are often more concerned about the business of ministry rather than tending to the lame or wounded sheep. They are prone to consider such use of their time as inefficient and prefer outsourcing hands-on care of the sheep to others. While achieving efficiency means being the most productive with the least amount of time, the efforts put forth often have the stench of human wisdom and selfish ambition. The principles of business efficiency may act as good lubrication for a well-oiled machine, but they are lousy salve for binding the hearts of the broken. It takes time to weep with those who weep and rejoice with those who rejoice. The compassion of Christ cannot be manufactured. It can only come as we see people through the same lens as our Lord. He was moved with compassion because he saw the people distressed and helpless, "like sheep having no shepherd" (Matt 9:36).

The shepherds were supposed to protect the sheep and mend their brokenness. However, God revealed through Ezekiel that the desire of the shepherds of Israel was only to feed themselves (Ezek 34:2–3). An improper lens is created when the shepherd's selfish desire supersedes his call to die to himself and live for the sheep. With selfish gain as the looking glass, brokenness is overlooked or distorted.

In the professional paradigm, shepherds too often refer the care of souls, divinely entrusted to them, to "caregivers" outside the church.

Unfortunately, some pastors have viewed soul care as beyond their skill set or job description, saying, "Those things should be left to the experts." However, these "professionals" tend to divide brokenness into secular categories, devoid of spiritual understanding.[7] Correspondingly, the Bible becomes irrelevant for binding the broken.

As representatives of Christ to the flock, we cannot claim to be unqualified in the very business for which our Savior called us. One could scarcely find an employee who would tell his boss that he was unqualified for a job that is his responsibility. The employee would do all he could to gain the necessary skills and abilities to perform the task for which he is accountable. The same could be said for shepherds. In order to be qualified to mend the broken, the shepherds do not need to be trained experts in psychology. Rather, in keeping with the classical tradition of pastoral care, shepherds should be deeply rooted in biblical anthropology and an appropriate application of God's Word.

Thomas Oden calls the pastor-as-shepherd imagery a "pivotal analogy."[8] In part, the analogy highlights the paradox of the shepherd as he leads through service. One should not be fooled into thinking the analogy has been replaced because it is outdated for the modern world. The problem is not that we are unable to understand the ancient analogy of a lowly shepherd but that we prefer the model of a business manager as more fitting to our modern context. The shepherd is not the leader due to his competence as an efficient administrator but rather in his competence to care. To claim the analogy as novelty or a bygone profession seems to be more convenient than necessary.

Superficial Remedies

A second threat to biblical shepherding is the influence of secular psychologies. The dependence of churches upon psychology should not be surprising, since this influence has been in our institutions of theological

---

[7] Cf. 1 Cor 2:14.

[8] Thomas Oden, *Pastoral Theology: Essentials of Ministry* (New York: Harper Collins, 1983), 49–54.

education for over 80 years.[9] Derek Tidball observes, "In the mid-twentieth century behavioral and social sciences seemed to mount a rescue bid by providing pastoral theology with the theoretical framework."[10] E. Brooks Holifield argues that, due to the influence of the social sciences in the last century, the understanding of salvation has drastically shifted from true gospel to self-realization. Psychology (both psychoanalytic and behavioral influences) has become the epistemological foundation upon which brokenness is explained. The popularity of these philosophies as a means to care for individuals has become a formidable foe for the minister who feels his contributions to be inadequate in such a specialized and psychologized world. A dangerous chasm has been created between Christian doctrine and practice.

The work of mending based on psychological thought is focused on the treatment of symptoms. If we seek to alleviate symptoms instead of causes, our care may provide temporary comfort but in the end, an artificial peace. Matthew Henry's commentary on Jer 8:4–12 sheds light on the attempt made by Ezekiel's shepherds to relieve without curing:

> They flattered people in their sins, and so flattered them into destruction. They pretended to be the physicians of the state, but knew not how to apply proper remedies to its growing maladies; they *healed them slightly*, killed the patient with palliative cures, silencing their fears and complaints with, "*Peace, peace*, all is well, and there is no danger," when the God of heaven was proceeding in his controversy with them, so that there could be no peace to them.[11]

---

[9] See Edward E. Thornton, *Professional Education for Ministry: A History of Clinical Pastoral Education* (Nashville: Abingdon Press, 1970); E. Brooks Holifield, *A History of Pastoral Care in America: From Salvation to Self-Realization* (Eugene, OR: Wipf & Stock, 1983); and T. Dale Johnson, "Professionalization of Pastoral Care within the Southern Baptist Convention: Gaines Dobbins and the Psychology of Religion," PhD dissertation, Southwestern Baptist Theological Seminary, 2014.

[10] Derek J. Tidball, *Skillful Shepherds: An Introduction to Pastoral Theology* (Grand Rapids: Zondervan Publishing, 1986), 13.

[11] Matthew Henry, *Matthew Henry's Commentary on the Whole Bible: Complete and Unabridged in One Volume* (Peabody, MA: Hendrickson, 1994).

The use of psychology was intended to explore and understand human nature and, in so doing, provide remedies to quiet the souls of men. In this model, the Christian paradigm becomes one of many means to gain a healthy personality. In humanistic psychology, guilt and shame are seen as unwanted symptoms of the human experience. The therapeutic cure is to rid ourselves of the symptoms of guilt and shame, without addressing the cause. The interpretation of man from secular and therapeutic sources can lead the theologian to think in terms of non-Christian causality and cure of souls.[12] Assessing someone based simply on symptoms is similar to feeling around in a dark room with the back of your hand. You may notice something is there, but discerning the details is impossible. Adding humanistic psychology to the lens of discernment only blurs one's perception of the heart.

To adapt the theories of Freud, Rogers, and Skinner to biblical truth seems odd. It could be argued that the only thing these men agreed on was that religion was a detriment for human psychological health. Knowing that these men denied the truth of the gospel, does it make sense to treat them as guides to spiritual health? Their methods merely manufacture victims of the environment, social order, heredity, or family. This mode of shepherding reduces Jesus to a cosmic psychologist who exists to refine coping skills or enlighten self-awareness. How we practice the care of the soul makes a fundamental statement about who we believe Jesus to be and the purpose for which He suffered.

Practices based on psychologies that are divorced from doctrine create an altar of pragmatism where Scripture is sacrificed. Ezekiel 34 is a call for shepherds to hold both doctrine and practice dearly. As God's under-shepherds, we model the care He has revealed in His Word. The earthly shepherd is to mimic the care promised by "the Chief Shepherd" (1 Pet 5:4) so that when He appears, the flock will know His voice and His ways.

In this climate of professionalization, extreme care must be taken toward a path that reinstates the full responsibility of the shepherd. The same diligence he has in preparing and delivering biblical messages to his people corporately should also pervade his ministry of the Word to individuals

---

[12] Wayne E. Oates, *The Religious Dimensions of Personality* (New York: Association Press, 1957), 48–49.

and families. Otherwise, he compromises his ability to lead the flock of God to comfort in times of grief, to hope in times of destitution, to righteousness in times of thirst, and to protection in times of attack.

The psychologist can only offer superficial remedies that merely imitate peace. The peace pursued through psychology is found within an individual in the power to self-actualize, build self-esteem, or control one's own behavior. The problem is that peace is not found within man or the will to change one's own actions. Peace is found in a person—the person the undershepherd is called to reflect: Jesus. He is the wonderful Counselor, the Prince of Peace, our refuge and very present help in time of trouble (Ps 46:1; Isa 9:6).

The modern context of pastoral theology has been muddled by the advent of the social sciences. Ezekiel 34 should be viewed as warning against the overreliance on social sciences to cure the soul. This chapter unveils a predictable conclusion for our use of the psychologies as our primary balm for binding. Ultimately, that sort of bandage for the broken soul is, at best, a temporary and superficial remedy. Are you the Lord's counselor, trying to supplement His wisdom to discern and cure the soul, or are you His servant following His instructions? If you and I are bondservants, then we trust the ointment given by the Master to cure.

The Rod and the Staff: Binding the Broken

In a home with six children we experience scrapes and bruises regularly. Imagine one of my children falling off his bicycle, resulting in a lesion on his head and cuts down his back. We take him to the doctor, and the doctor gives him a tube of salve but does not help him apply it on the wounds. The child has the ointment necessary to heal and protect from infection but is void of the ability to use it properly. He needs someone who will actually care for his wounds and not just describe the treatment.

Shepherds have the ability to apply the balm of God's Word to the hard-to-reach places of the human heart. The wise pastor, following the example of the good Shepherd, administers the light of God's Word to the fleshly passions hidden in the dark crevices of the human heart.

Jesus Binds the Brokenhearted

Sin, original and personal, is the culprit of the brokenness of man. The first sin of Adam and Eve, which resulted in the brokenness of the whole world, was due to their rejection of God's Word. The crafty serpent asked our first parents, "Did God really say . . . ?" That small speck of doubt and the action built upon it caused the groaning of creation in shattered and shamed hearts. One lesson from Eden is that God's Word protects human hearts from self-destruction. Christ was promised as the Seed coming to crush the cause of brokenness (Gen 3:15). His purpose was to glorify the Father, and it pleased the Father to crush the iniquity that caused the brokenness.

God has not forgotten the brokenhearted. Rather, He has demonstrated His care by sending Christ to bandage those who have been broken. Jesus was the long-awaited One who came to crush the curse of sin and death. He is the good Shepherd foretold in Ezek 34:16 and revealed in John 10. Jesus is the balm that cures the broken heart and the bread of heaven that sustains them.

In Jeremiah 8, the shepherds of Israel were unsuccessful in healing the brokenness of God's people. The chapter concludes with a series of rhetorical questions:

Is there no balm in Gilead?
Is there no physician there?
Why then is there no recovery
For the health of the daughter of My people?

God was revealing that the remedy for the broken heart is to be found in the "balm in Gilead." Jesus as the fulfillment of Isaiah 61, the One who binds the brokenhearted and the good Shepherd of Ezek 34:16, offers the medicinal balm that heals the wounded heart. Matthew Henry states that, "The blood of Christ is balm in Gilead, his Spirit is the physician there, both sufficient, all-sufficient."[13]

The psalmist wrote, "The LORD is near to those who have a broken heart / And saves such as have a contrite spirit" (Ps 34:18). He sent His

---

[13] Henry, *Matthew Henry's Commentary on the Whole Bible,* Jer 8:13–22.

Son in order that the brokenhearted may be healed. Sometimes His refining work is designed to crucify those parts of us that breed our brokenness. Paul confesses in Romans, "Oh wretched man that I am! Who will deliver me from this body of death?" (Rom 7:24). But God, in Christ, mends our broken hearts. He is aiding our exit from the perpetual cycle of brokenness propagated by our fleshly desires.

As the Word of God transforms your heart, you are able to reflect the character of God to the people. The Word of God through the Holy Spirit of God in God's shepherd becomes the bread of God for the people of God.[14] The Word of God upon the hearts of men restores the fullness of the *imago Dei*. A soul is mended toward its original design to the degree that it rests upon the precepts of God. The heart then adequately reflects the character of God as a display of His glory. This is the work of Christ, the mender of the brokenhearted. The Holy Spirit works in us to transform us into the image of Christ, the One who reflected God perfectly on the earth.

As the good Shepherd, Christ works to bind the hearts of those who are broken. The tool He uses is the Word of God. The psalmist declared, "The law of the LORD is perfect, converting the soul" (Ps 19:7). The soul is brought back from evil and turned again to God. Jesus, speaking of His own body says, "Take, eat; this is My body which is broken for you" (1 Cor 11:24). He was broken so that we do not have to be. Jesus as the suffering servant in Psalm 22 is the Shepherd who restores our soul in Psalm 23. The Lord heals the brokenhearted and binds up the wounds of those who trust in Him.

Binding Is a Duty of the Shepherd

The task of binding the broken has been demonstrated for us by the chief Shepherd. In Ezek 34:16, God promised that He would bind up the broken. Jesus, "the image of the invisible God" (Col 1:15), accomplished the work promised by the Father as the good Shepherd (John 10). Luke

---

[14] However, the shepherds of Ezekiel's day were using the people of God as bread for themselves.

4:18 reveals Christ's fulfillment of Isaiah 61, the One who would bind up the brokenhearted.[15]

Now God has entrusted that task to His shepherds. However, when the shepherd's eyes are fixed on his own gain, there is very little room to see the brokenness of the sheep. Rather than "hearing a word" from the mouth of God, the shepherds God rebuked in Ezekiel 34 chose an alternate path (v. 3). In the end, the sheep were left broken and unbound.

To argue that the ministry of a shepherd should be distinctly biblical ought to be obvious. The messengers of God are not called to success, but to faithfulness. Richard Baxter said, "A minister is not to be merely a public preacher, but to be known as a counsellor [*sic*] for their souls, as the physician is for their bodies, and the lawyer for their estates."[16]

The Word of God held as preeminent in a corporate gathering ought to take no less of a position in our ministry to individuals and families. Too often, in their work of shepherding, pastors neglect the power of the tool they proclaim as effectual in their preaching, often deferring to pragmatic techniques in order to soothe the broken soul.

The voices of undershepherds are often overshadowed by the consistent and growing pitch of the culture. The common enticements to believe in a world dominated by a temporal perspective often blind, bind, and break because they are alluring to the fleshly desires that war against the Spirit of God within us. Brokenness frequently occurs as a shift in anchors from the miniature hopes in which people place their trust. As those temporal hopes come crashing down, and sometimes with great force and thrust upon the soul, only the truths of the Word represent the lasting hope that comforts our souls.

As the Word of God comforts, it also protects. Souls are apt to break upon the false and rigid hopes found in the temporary world. Souls holding

---

[15] Psalms 38 and 147 also combine *shabar* (Hb., "be broken") with *leb* (Hb., "heart") so as to express more clearly the heart as the object of the brokenness. The point is that the work of the shepherd is to minister to those broken in heart, not to the neglect of the body, the symptoms of which may be outward expressions of inner pain. The Scripture indicates that we express emotions and outward behavior from dispositions within. So it is proper that the ministry to an individual be focused on the inner person of the heart. Only the Word of God, written and living, by the Spirit of Christ, can discern and change the heart.

[16] Richard Baxter, *The Reformed Pastor*, ed. William Brown (Carlisle, PA: The Banner of Truth Trust, 1999), 96.

fast to the promises and precepts of God's Word will be anchored to the eternal hope that Christ will make all things new. The heart is then protected from the enticing "eye candy" with its worldly appeal, which inevitably leads to "cavities" in the heart. If we attempt to mend hearts by a different means, then we must admit that brokenness is caused by something outside of the realm of God's ability to heal.

Ezekiel's accusation that the shepherds would be judged for not binding the broken is indicative of their responsibility to God and to those whom they were called to lead. As Timothy Laniak suggests, "Abusing others was an expression of the arrogant assumption that power is primarily privilege rather than responsibility."[17] Neglect of shepherds to minister the Word of God to the brokenhearted is abuse of the sheep in the eyes of God. The shepherd's disregard does not remove the fact that he is a shepherd; it simply means he is not a good one. It means he is a hireling simply seeking a selfish sum instead of sacrificial service reflecting the selflessness of Christ.

Your willingness to be involved should not be based on your availability or ability but on the need of the sheep. Neither the level of inconvenience nor your belief that someone's need does not match your skill set is among the criteria used in discerning your involvement. Working with the sheep often presents difficulties that press your known limitations. Yet, in human weakness Christ is strong. We must not be afraid to engage in situations that supersede our earthly ability. Here Christ gets due credit for proper care as the wonderful Counselor beyond human wit or ability.

The degree to which the shepherd reflects Christ in his character is the same degree to which he reflects Christ in his ministry to the broken. The character of the shepherd is unveiled in moments when the flock is distressed. Bad character results in a superficial patchwork of the broken believer. God's message to the shepherds in Ezekiel 34 reveals His concern with the methods they chose to care for His sheep. The pragmatic tips for pastoral duties may work fine in a world of tolerance and relativism,

---

[17] Timothy S. Laniak, *Shepherds After My Own Heart: Pastoral Traditions and Leadership in the Bible*, New Studies in Biblical Theology 15 (Downers Grove, IL: InterVarsity Press, 2006), 149.

but delicate souls require a healing balm in the form of God's revelation lived out through earthen vessels of God's chosen ministers.

Assessing the Broken

The shepherd cannot assess a broken spirit from a distance. God demonstrated the importance of nearness in ministry when He sent Christ to dwell among us. Shepherding means that pastors weep with those who weep and rejoice with those who rejoice. It means our hands will get dirty as we minister to those who have been left broken on the side of the road. Like the Samaritan's ministry to the man in need, our care—as well as knowing our sheep well enough to mend their ailing hearts—will cost resources, time, and energy (Luke 10:25–37). Our assessments should involve both compassionate listening and gracious discernment.

Compassionate Listening

Compassion cannot be mustered by human will. True compassion, the type that motivated Christ, is produced by seeing the multitudes from God's perspective. He saw the lost world and what their fate would be apart from the mercies of God. Compassion grows in the shepherd by seeing others through the lens of God's mercy shown at the cross.

Pastoral care has long taught the value of listening. Since the 1940s, the Rogerian model of active listening has been employed in the practice of pastoral care.[18] However, this is not compassionate listening; it is only

---

[18] While the Rogerian movement grew to prominence in the 1950s, Carl Rogers's influence among those teaching pastoral theology and pastoral care was well established in the late 1940s. Holifield demonstrates the influence of Rogers and others growing progressively post World War II (*A History of Pastoral Care in America*, 259–76). Also see Seward Hiltner, *Pastoral Counseling* (Nashville: Abingdon-Cokesbury Press, 1949), 29, 1045; Holifield, *Preface to Pastoral Theology*, chap. 6, n. 25. Hiltner demonstrates the rapid growth of literature in the pastoral care movement, naming Carroll A. Wise, Charles F. Kemp, Carl J. Scherzer, Paul B. Maves, A. Graham Ikin, Russell L. Dicks, and Richard Cabot as primary contributors. For a clear understanding of the new pastoral theology also see, Leroy Aden, "Rogerian Therapy and Optimal Pastoral Counseling," in *The New Shape of Pastoral Theology: Essays in Honor of Seward Hiltner*, ed. William B. Oglesby, Jr. (Nashville: Abingdon Press, 1969), 263–81; Johnson, "The Professionalization of Pastoral Care Within the Southern Baptist Convention," 39–42, 159–62; David Powlison, *The*

hearing. There is only "unconditional positive regard" for every desire the person expresses. But this is little more than "the blind leading the blind into a pit" (Matt 15:14). To listen compassionately is to hear a story through the framework of Scripture. It is to listen for unbiblical thinking leading to unbiblical actions and resulting in brokenness. The willingness to listen for unbiblical thinking in order to speak biblical truth in love is a demonstration of compassion-driven listening.

Gracious Discernment

Compassionate listening should always lead to gracious discernment. Brokenness should be categorized biblically in order to assess the problem accurately. As problems are defined and understood biblically, the affections can then be sorted in order to arrive at a treatment. Allow me to illustrate the danger of discerning through a faulty foundation.

At Christmastime my family makes the long trek from Texas to Florida. During the drive we enjoy listening to all the classic Christmas songs. My children sing at the top of their lungs, but I have noticed that they occasionally belt out different words than the artist. The word they think is in the song is not in the song at all. The kids sing what they have always heard, but they have not had the vocabulary to hear the word correctly. So, they sing these wrong words with confidence, trusting what they think they have heard so many times. Shepherds may make the same mistake if their ears are not tuned to God's Word.

Shepherds must take care to measure all the things they hear and see by the only true gauge—the Scriptures. If the heart of the shepherd is not tuned to the truth of Scripture, then important pieces of the broken soul will pass by unnoticed. The shepherd is sure to misdiagnose and mistreat the broken soul with superficial remedies. As Calvin states, "God's word is a *discerner* . . . for it brings the light of knowledge to the mind of man as it were from a labyrinth, where it was held before entangled."[19] Mature shepherds "have their senses exercised to discern both good and evil"

Biblical Counseling Movement: History and Context (Greensboro, NC: New Growth Press, 2010), 4–5.

[19] John Calvin, *Commentaries on the Epistle of Paul the Apostle to the Hebrews,* trans. John Owen (Edinburgh: The Calvin Translation Society, 1853), 104.

(Heb 5:14). The deep recesses of the heart are no match for the light of God's word because all things are open and made bare before His eyes (Heb 4:12–13).

Sorting the Affections[20]

Man's actions are not neutral; neither does he have a neutral thought. Proverbs 4:23 and Matt 15:18 declare that the heart of man produces the words and actions that come out in living life. Since words and deeds are produced by beliefs and passions in the heart of man, every word and deed has a corresponding spiritual significance. First Corinthians 10:31 demonstrates the spiritual significance associated with all tasks of men, even the ordinary tasks of eating and drinking. Put simply, everything one thinks, says, or does makes a statement about God. So we listen in order to discern what the person's thoughts and actions are proclaiming about God. At points where those thoughts and actions are contrary to the character and truth revealed about God in the Scripture, a portion of the soul's infection has been identified.

---

[20] Physical ailments are scarcely, if ever, divorced from soulish responses. Therefore, we have a responsibility, even in cases we believe to be biological in nature, to minister to both body and soul in hopes to bind the brokenness the flock has acquired in suffering. The Word of God is not intended to be a magic potion or spellbinding book of sayings. The Scriptures provide proper perspective in affliction. Modern medicine, especially in psychiatry, categorizes various types of suffering into divisions the pastor feels inadequate to address. Any hope in medicine, however, is only temporary since the Fall will run its course with every man. Not even modern medicine can alleviate the death effects of the Fall. Our physical suffering and sickness must be kept in proper perspective. Sin is the problem, death is the accurate prognosis, and physical sufferings are symptoms of the decay of the mortal body. At some point the Adam death will prevail—a fact that must not be lost with the hope-filled mirage created by modern medicine. The only true hope to mend the brokenness that leads to the inevitable is that Christ has been resurrected as the firstfruits of those who believe (1 Cor 15:20). This world is not our lasting city; we seek one that is to come, and Jesus will one day make all things new. The promise of Jesus's resurrected life is the only cure and legitimate hope for the inherited death of Adam. Shepherd, do not allow your people to lose perspective. Minister the Word so that their affections are reoriented to the world to come. This will help bind the fear and uncertainty that so easily entangles as it seeps into their hearts during momentary affliction. Consistently remind them of the eternal weight of glory; it is proper salve in physical affliction and the soul vexation produced by the reality of a perishable body.

A man's words and actions over time reveal his affections. Human shepherds do not easily interpret the affections of men because they see through a glass darkly. But, Scripture affirms that "[T]he LORD does not see as man sees for man looks at the outward appearance, but the LORD looks at the heart" (1 Sam 16:7). The tool of the shepherd is the Word of God because it is the only thing that can lay bare the human heart. Through the lens of Scripture, the shepherd can more accurately categorize the wounded.

Application of the therapeutic medicine of the Word depends on how the wounds of the sheep are categorized. First Thessalonians 5:14 reveals three such categories. First, the shepherd is to *admonish the rebellious heart*. A sheep that has been wounded due to his stubbornness and conscious rejection of God's Word should be admonished. This person is a cause of his own brokenness, and the truth upon his heart can stop the bleeding wound.

Second, the shepherd is called to *encourage the fainthearted*. Someone who is weary in well-doing could be accurately placed in this category. The faint of heart would crumble if the remedy of admonition were applied. In this case it is necessary to share words of encouragement that build them up and bring grace to him that hears (Eph 4:29).

Finally, shepherds are called to *help those who are weak*. Paul tells us to bear with the failings of the weak (Rom 15:1). We are to demonstrate patience and teach those who are acting out of ignorance or immaturity. Before I spank my children for any offense, I must first make sure that they clearly understand expectations. If my child willingly disobeys, my response is different than at times when he may be acting out of ignorance. I am more patient with the child who lacks the knowledge necessary to obey. The same is true as we shepherd those who are weak in the faith.

Loving Affirmation

The work of the pastor is prevention and cure. He is to be both the general practitioner and the emergency room doctor. His application of the Word of God as a salve is to be broad to prevent the soul from stumbling. But, he must also make application of particular doses of ointment to the souls with seeping wounds.

Treatment is determined by the assessment and categorization of the wound. All should be spoken in love, but not all things are spoken in the same way. For example, the way in which Christ spoke truth in love to the Pharisees was quite different than the way he spoke to wounded sinners. Paul speaks with kind affection to the Corinthian church in his second letter because they had humbly received the word of God. Yet, Paul's tone is different to those in Galatia who were being persuaded by the Judaizers. All of the truth was spoken in love, but not all with a tone of tolerance.

At times the flesh becomes so festered that deep infections of the soul must be lanced in order to prevent a hardened heart. The only tool sharp enough to pierce the depth of the infectious heart is "the sword of the Spirit, which is the word of God" (Eph 6:17). The skilled physician of the soul is not one who dispenses theories and methodologies birthed in humanism and depleted of the supernatural. Rather, the making of a good caretaker is one conformed to the image of the wonderful Counselor and Prince of Peace. In Jesus "we see the perfect balance of comforting the afflicted and afflicting the comfortable that is the shepherd's task."[21]

The pain inflicted by the Spirit's sword allows for healing to begin in the soul, but that is not the only way to mend a broken heart. Some broken hearts are the result of blunt force trauma in our chaotic world. The curse of creation wears on these bodies of clay, and often we are wounded by shards of other broken people. In these cases, salve must be consistently applied to heal the open wound. Both treatments rely upon the precision of the Word of God. One cure is the use of a sharp tool to release the pressure of infectious and sinful desires. The other antidote is the gentle application of the balm of the Word to a tender surface.

The task of the shepherd is to make everyone complete in Christ. As a person is conformed to the image of Christ, he is able to bring glory to the Father through suffering. The shepherd is called to speak truth to the flock so that each member of the body can mature in Christ. Growth in Christ is the greatest stabilizer of the human heart to withstand the winds and waves of trickery and deceitful scheming of the enemy.

---

[21] Iain Daguid, *Ezekiel*, NIVAC (Grand Rapids: Zondervan, 1999), 400.

As shepherds, we desire for our people to have peace, but peace is not manufactured by human hands. Peace is a production of the Spirit in the hearts of men. Therefore, we must work with urgency to expose those who are broken to the sword of the Spirit. Ultimately, we know that "[a]ny attempt to produce love, joy, peace, endurance and so forth apart from the Spirit of God is reliance upon strategies that are in competition with God."[22] To look to anything, apart from God, to make life work is to forsake God. Shepherds want their sheep to look away from themselves and to fix their gaze on Christ, the healer of broken hearts, because "any change that will ultimately help man must move him away from autonomy and must move him toward dependence upon his Creator."[23] The words of C. S. Lewis should encourage us to teach men to be satisfied in God:

> God made us: invented us as a man invents an engine. A car is made to run on gasoline, and it would not run properly on anything else. Now God designed the human machine to run on Himself. He Himself is the fuel our spirits were designed to burn, or the food our spirits were designed to feed on. There is no other. That is why it is just no good asking God to make us happy in our own way without bothering about religion. God cannot give us happiness and peace apart from Himself, because it is not there. There is no such thing.[24]

Speaking the truth in love is not telling the sheep to "take two scriptures and call me in the morning." As Ichabod Spencer asserts, "There are *some* scripture arrows, which we should always have in our quiver, because they are sure to hit."[25] However, we must be able to use the Word of the Lord with precision in order to address the delicate issues of the soul. Pierre and Reju accurately express the importance of a shepherd's care to be biblical: "The goal is to call people to faith in a way that specifically

---

[22] Jim Berg, *Changed into His Image: God's Plan for Transforming Your Life* (Greenville, SC: Bob Jones University Press, 1999), 15.

[23] Ibid., 68.

[24] C. S. Lewis, *Mere Christianity* (Old Tappan: Macmillan Publishing Company, Inc., 1979), 54.

[25] Ichabod S. Spencer, *A Pastor's Sketches: Or, Conversations with Anxious Inquirers Respecting the Way of Salvation*, 4th ed. (New York: M. W. Dodd, 1851), 119.

addresses their heart responses, since faith alone is the means by which a person responds rightly (Heb. 11:6, 13–16; 12:1–2). And faith comes through hearing the word of Christ (Rom. 10:17)."[26] Faith builds hope. Hope is produced by the Spirit through perseverance in tribulations. As Paul reminded us, "Even though our outward man is perishing, yet the inward man is being renewed" as we hope in things that are eternal (2 Cor 4:16). This hope we have is an anchor to the soul, built upon faith in Christ. This hope is steadfast and sure and will not put us to shame.[27]

The shepherds who do not bind the broken from God's perspective are foolish. They may have convinced the world or even themselves that they are wise, but they have become fools by neglecting the work that reflects the character of God. Their time and techniques are spent on superficial remedies that seem wise to the world but are worthless in God's eyes. In contrast, the true shepherd demonstrates the character of God as he lays down his life for the sheep. He is entrusting his life into the hands of the Father, whose character is good and compassionate. We must not neglect giving our lives for the sheep simply out of fear that we will not get a just reward.[28] We must not abandon the only true ointment that binds the broken. Instead, we must hear the word of the Lord through the prophet Jeremiah:

Thus says the LORD:

"Stand by the ways and see,
And ask for the old paths, where the good way is,
And walk in it;
Then you will find rest for your souls." (Jer 6:16)

---

[26] Jeremy Pierre and Deepak Reju, *The Pastor and Counseling: The Basics of Shepherding Members in Need* (Wheaton, IL: Crossway, 2015), 50–51.
[27] Heb 6:17–20; Rom 5:5; 9:33; Ps 119:116.
[28] Zech 11:15–17.

CHAPTER 6

The Shepherd Who Protects the Sheep

Malcolm Yarnell

The shepherd who faithfully shepherds the flock is a rich metaphor used by God's elect to express His loving care for His people. The shepherd who neglects or abuses the flock and causes it to scatter, while he is busy pursuing his own welfare, is a perfect metaphor for what a leader should not be. Both of these metaphors, the good shepherd and the evil shepherd, are prominent in Ezekiel 34. While the outworking of their actions is discussed in Ezekiel, the driving forces behind their actions, vis-à-vis the flock that God has placed in their care, is made clear only in the New Testament. A journey through the Hebrew Bible and into the New Testament will help place Ezekiel 34 within the divine economy that Scripture reveals. Ultimately, God Himself must come as Messiah in order to reveal the Shepherd who rightly shepherds the flock of God.

Ezekiel 34:5–8 in Historical Context

As has already been seen in previous chapters, God holds shepherds accountable for the care of the sheep. Verses 5–8 in Ezekiel 34 are the primary concern for this chapter, but for a proper interpretation, these verses must be placed within their original prophetic context as well as within the

canon of the Christian Bible. Verses 5–8 form what we believe to be the
divine prosecutor's particular indictment and preliminary judgment in His
case against the evil shepherds of Israel. Ezekiel 34 contains two separate
yet related indictments. As previously addressed in the introduction, the
first indictment—against the evil shepherds of the people (vv. 1–9)—concludes with a judgment against the evil shepherds (v. 10) and a promise to
restore the flock with a new shepherd (vv. 11–16). The second indictment
concerns the stronger sheep that are abusing the weaker sheep (vv. 17–19).
The second indictment also concludes with a judgment against the evil
sheep (vv. 20–21) and a promise to restore the flock with Yahweh and His
messianic servant caring for them (vv. 22–31).[1]

The prophet's ministry occurred during the period when Ezekiel was
among the Judeans who had been deported from Jerusalem to Babylon.
While his exile began with King Jehoiachin's surrender of his own people
in 598–597 BC, Ezekiel's ministry began with God's calling of him in
Babylon in 593 BC (Ezek 1:1). His ministry did not conclude until some-
time after 571 BC (29:17).[2] The final fall and destruction of Jerusalem
under King Zedekiah in 586 BC was the major contemporary event in
Israel's public history and was similarly significant in Ezekiel's personal
history (33:21–22). The recording of Jerusalem's destruction in Ezekiel
33 provided not only a pivotal historical transition for the people; Jerusalem's final capture brought a pivotal shift in the theological ministry of the
prophet Ezekiel. Prior to the fall of Jerusalem, Ezekiel's prophecies were
focused on destroying the false covenantal theology of the people and their
leaders. After 586 BC, Ezekiel emphasized God's promises to restore His
people.[3]

The literary placement of the indictments in chapter 34 after the fall
of Jerusalem in Ezekiel 33 probably does not indicate its precise historical context. In my opinion, the oracle likely was delivered immediately

---

[1] For an alternative though conducive ordering of the indictments, see Leslie C. Allen,
Ezekiel 20–48, WBC (Dallas, TX: Word Books, 1990), 158–59.

[2] Christopher T. Begg, "Ezekiel, The Book of," in *The Oxford Illustrated Companion
to the Bible*, ed. Bruce M. Metzger and Michael D. Coogan (New York: Oxford University
Press, 2003), 84.

[3] Daniel I. Block, *The Book of Ezekiel, Chapters 25–48*, NICOT (Grand Rapids: Eerdmans, 1998), 271.

before or contemporaneous with the fall of Jerusalem. Ezekiel relayed the judgment of God against the king as the shepherd and against the leading nobility as the "fat sheep" whom God had placed over the people of Judah. Despite its message of judgment against evil leaders, the literary placement of Ezekiel 34 at the very beginning of the "salvation oracles" of the prophet[4] definitely indicates its overwhelmingly hopeful content. The prophecy did not bring good tidings for the privileged shepherds and fat sheep of Israel, of course. But for the common people, who had been neglected and abused by the same shepherds and fat sheep, the oracles would have been very comforting. There is hope for the future beyond the horrors of rule under both Israelite kings and Babylonian overlords.

The Shepherd of the Sheep as Hebrew Metaphor

The theological and political content of the prophecy in Ezekiel 34 is profoundly important, not only for ancient Israel but also for the people of God today. A review of the progress of the use of the metaphor of the shepherd (Hb. *ra'ah*; Gk. *poimēn*) with the sheep (Hb. *tso'n*; Gk. *probata*) within the biblical canon is helpful for understanding why the shepherds in Ezek 34:5–8 were brought under condemnation by God. It also provides suggestions regarding what this means for the people of God and their leaders today.

Ezekiel has been noted as a careful reader of the biblical tradition.[5] When he offers a complex judgment on the leaders of Jerusalem through the metaphor of shepherding, he is thus drawing upon a longstanding tradition. The tradition is evident not only in the Old Testament but also in many of the cultures of the ancient Near East, stretching back into the Sumerian period. The prologue to the Code of Hammurabi, for instance, describes the king as the divinely called "shepherd." Hammurabi was given the responsibility "to promote the welfare of the people," "to cause

---

[4] "A salvation oracle is a prophetic pronouncement of deliverance from a stressful situation and the restoration of total peace and harmony" (Ibid., 268–69). Block borrows the term from Claus Westermann, who speaks of such prophets as *Heilsworte*, "oracles," or more literally, "saving words." Cp. Claus Westermann, "Zur Erforschung und zum Verständnis der prophetischen Heilsworte," *ZAW* 98 (1986): 1–13.

[5] Begg, "Ezekiel," 86.

justice to prevail in the land," and "to destroy the wicked and the evil, that the strong might not oppress the weak."[6] Daniel Block summarizes the use of the shepherd motif to describe similarly the roles of kings in the Assyrian, Babylonian, and Egyptian contexts.[7]

Rikk E. Watts locates the Bible's opening use of the shepherd metaphor in Num 27:17, which relays the concern of Moses for a proper successor to lead the people of Israel.[8] Andreas J. Köstenberger locates the basis for John's use of the metaphor likewise.[9] In this poignant episode toward the end of his life, as he is surveying the promised land from afar (Num 27:12–23), Moses asks the Lord to provide a man to lead the community to go out and come back, presumably assaying to war then back to the safety of the camp. He caps the request with a metaphor of concern for the people not to become "like sheep which have no shepherd" (Num 27:17).

The Lord responds that Moses should lay hands upon Joshua, "a man in whom is the Spirit" (Num 27:18). The qualifying presence of *ruach* (Hb. "spirit") in Joshua was evinced through previous exploits in which Joshua demonstrated his loyalty to the Lord (cp. Exod 17; 24; 31; 33; Num 11; 13–14). "This spirit was not something that now came upon Joshua, or was temporary; it already existed in Joshua and was the basis of God's choice of him."[10] (In Deut 34:9, Joshua is also described as possessing "the spirit of wisdom.") The subsequent laying on of hands by Moses was to be done before the assembled people while consulting with the Lord. This was the public means of conveying a sacred authority upon Joshua (Num 27:18–23). The public consulting of the Lord through "the judgment of the Urim" indicated God's certain approval of Joshua (v. 21), but the conferring through Moses explicitly of only "some of" (Hb. *min*, lit. "part of")

---

[6] "The Code of Hammurabi," trans. Theophile J. Meek, in *Ancient Near Eastern Texts Relating to the Old Testament*, ed. J. B. Pritchard, 3rd ed. (Princeton: Princeton University Press, 1969), 164.

[7] Block, *The Book of Ezekiel*, 281.

[8] Rikk E. Watts, "Mark," in *Commentary on the New Testament Use of the Old Testament*, ed. G. K. Beale and D. A. Carson (Grand Rapids: Baker Academic, 2007), 158–61.

[9] Andreas J. Köstenberger, "John," in *Commentary on the New Testament Use of the Old Testament*, ed. G. K. Beale and D. A. Carson (Grand Rapids: Baker Academic, 2007), 462.

[10] Timothy R. Ashley, *The Book of Numbers*, NICOT (Grand Rapids: Eerdmans, 1993), 552.

the latter's authority indicated also a limitation on Joshua (v. 20). Moses was then to render a commission to Joshua in the public assembly (v. 23).

Among the important theological elements of this politically formative episode for setting aside the shepherds of the people of God are:

- the existence of a publicly demonstrable and standing spirituality in the shepherd;
- indication of divine approval through the laying on of hands by another spiritual leader himself, acting under divine command;
- explicit identification of the limitation and derivation of the authority of the new shepherd;
- identification of the people of God, through the charge, as important witnesses to and the intended beneficiaries of the ministry of the shepherd.[11]

The metaphor of "sheep which have no shepherd" was applied in the prophecy of Micaiah ben Imlah against Ahab, the king of Israel (1 Kgs 22:17; cp. 2 Chr 18:16). When Ahab subsequently died in battle, the army of Israel, as Micaiah prophesied, was "scattered" from the field of battle in defeat (1 Kgs 22:36). Rabbinic commentary upon this text identifies the scattering of the people of God as coming about due to the lack of wisdom and understanding within their leader.[12] If Moses and Joshua are the early exemplars for what a good shepherd is like, Ahab is the late exemplar for an evil shepherd.

David, on the other hand, is presented as successfully "leading out" and "bringing in" the people (2 Sam 5:2; cp. 1 Chr 11:2). This same mixed metaphor, which draws upon both pastoral and military imagery, is first applied to Joshua in Num 27:17. Therefore, Moses—through Joshua—is the good shepherd who begins the conquest of the promised land, while David is the good shepherd who completes the conquest (cp. Ps 78:12–20,

---

[11] Michael Walzer, a prominent Jewish political philosopher, notes that while the ancient Hebrew people should not be conceived in modern terms as citizens, the leaders of Israel were yet responsible to God for the people's well-being. Walzer, *In God's Shadow: Politics in the Hebrew Bible* (New Haven, CT: Yale University Press, 2012), 12–13.

[12] Watts, "Mark," 160.

70–72).[13] It is instructive that the two most prominent Israelite leaders historically, Moses and David, served as humble shepherds to literal animal flocks (Exod 3:1; 1 Sam 16:11–12) before becoming the great shepherds of the flock of God in the Old Testament.

Ezekiel was not the only prophet to draw upon the shepherd metaphor to prophesy the judgment of evil leaders of Israel. His older contemporary, Jeremiah, declaimed Judah's leaders, "Woe to the shepherds who destroy and scatter the sheep of My pasture!" (Jer 23:1; cp. 10:21; Mic 5:5; Zech 10:2–3; 11:3–8). The judgment and replacement of the evil shepherds is poetically appropriated through the use of *paqad* in Jeremiah 23. *Paqad* has a range of pastoral meanings, including "attend to," "go to see," and "take care of," as well as "appoint," "call to account," and "avenge."[14] Because the shepherds who were called to shepherd the people of God (Jer 23:2a) have not "attended to" the people of God, then God will in turn "attend to" the shepherds (Jer 23:2b). However, like Ezekiel, Jeremiah does not merely declaim evil leaders, he promises that God will raise up good shepherds who will properly shepherd his flock (Jer 23:4). Immediately afterwards, Jeremiah invokes the promise of a messianic figure who will "raise to David a Branch of righteousness" (Jer 23:5a). This "Messiah" (of Aramaic derivation; cp. Gk. *Christos*) will reign wisely as king and administer justice and righteousness in the land (Jer 23:5b). He will save Judah and will cause Israel to dwell in security (Jer 23:6).

Isaiah also utilizes the shepherd imagery. And, as in Jeremiah, God Himself will act toward His people as a shepherd. In the role of a victorious warrior returning to the home of His people from afar (Isa 40:9–10), the Lord will arrive to "feed his flock like a shepherd" (Isa 40:11a). To those outside his flock, the Lord is a fierce opponent, but to those inside, the Lord is a protective presence. "He will gather the lambs with His arm, / And carry them in His bosom" (Isa 40:11b). Not only is He a protective presence, the Lord is a comforting presence to the most vulnerable of His people, demonstrating sensitivity to their critical needs. He will "gently lead those who are with young" (Isa 40:11c). Isaiah's ease of transition

---

[13] Ibid., 159.

[14] J. A. Thompson, *The Book of Jeremiah*, NICOT (Grand Rapids: Eerdmans, 1980), 487.

from bloody warrior to gentle caregiver may astonish the contemporary reader, for the multivalent tasks of the ancient shepherd challenge what has been called the modern Western "feminization of Christianity."[15]

Prophets like Isaiah, Jeremiah, and Ezekiel were not the only ones who applied the metaphor of shepherd to the Lord. In Psalm 23, David demonstrates how the Lord as shepherd relates personally to His sheep. The rich associational quality of the term to David came through his own youthful occupation as a shepherd (1 Sam 16:11–12; cp. Ps 78:70–72). The shepherd was a basic component in the ancient Israelite economy. In the constant search for food in a dry climate, the flock would have to range widely, often far from home into the wild. This challenge made the sheep highly vulnerable to carnivorous animals, natural disaster, and accidental harm. The shepherd needed to monitor the sheep, protect them, heal them, and gather them into the temporary shelter of a fold after the day's grazing. The sheep were constantly dependent upon the ministrations of the shepherd. The sheep knew the direction for provision through hearing the unique tenor of their own shepherd's voice. The sheep, alas, were most vulnerable when scattered beyond the reach of their shepherd's care. "Without the shepherd the sheep were hopeless."[16]

David understood well the utter reliance of the sheep upon the shepherd, and he understood that, as a man, he was utterly dependent upon the Lord God. "The LORD is my shepherd" brought with it a personal comfort that God would lead David through places with verdant pasture and quiet water (Ps 23:1–2). However, during the journey, there were also places that reeked of fear—even death, but God had always and always would guide him on "the paths of righteousness" (v. 3). Also like a shepherd, Yahweh used His correcting rod and His guiding staff to "comfort" David (vv. 3–4). In the end, David looked forward to returning to the justice, safety, and provision of "the house of the Lord," when the dangers of the long journey through the wilderness would be complete (Ps 23:6).

---

[15] A controversial exposition of this phenomenon may be found in Leon J. Podles, *The Church Impotent: The Feminization of Christianity* (Dallas, TX: Spence Publishing, 1999). See also Charlotte Allen's scathing response to Podles's treatment of history though grudging admission of the problem in her review in *Theology Today* 58 (2001), 464–68.

[16] P. L. Garber, "Sheep, Shepherd," in *The International Standard Bible Encyclopedia*, rev. ed., ed. Geoffrey W. Bromiley (Grand Rapids: Eerdmans, 1979–1988), 4:464.

The Good Shepherd in the New Testament

In the New Testament the full theological meaning of the shepherd and sheep metaphor is manifest. And it is through sharp relief with the good Shepherd that the depth of depravity of the evil shepherds indicted in Ezek 34:5–8 becomes apparent. While Ezekiel, like David, Jeremiah, and Isaiah before him, applied the metaphor of the shepherd to the Lord, the Pharisees looked upon shepherds as scandalous due to their class and reputation as being untrustworthy. They discriminated legally against shepherds and were shocked that Psalm 23 applied this term to the Lord.[17] Over against this rabbinic distaste, Jesus Christ spoke positively about shepherds and even applied the metaphor to Himself: "I am the good shepherd" (John 10:14).

According to the Gospel of John's representation of Jesus, what marks a good shepherd as opposed to a "thief" (John 10:10) or a "hireling" (John 10:12–13) is the shepherd's willingness to give his life for the sheep (John 10:11). The novel idea introduced here in Jesus's teaching (John 10:15, 17), standing in contrast to the Pharisaic denunciation of shepherds and with no contemporary cultural parallel, is that the true shepherd is going to suffer "a voluntary and vicarious death for the flock."[18] Moreover, Jesus claims not only that He, as the good Shepherd, will lay down his life for his sheep, but also that He has the power to take it up again (John 10:18). The true shepherd has the will to die vicariously and the power to arise victoriously.

Jesus's teaching in this regard brings sense to the cryptic sayings of Zechariah 13. Moses had feared that the sheep of Israel would be scattered without a shepherd (Num 27:17), and Ezekiel taught that the scattering of the sheep of Israel was an evil result of evil shepherds (Ezek 34:5–6). Indeed, Ezekiel mentions the scattering of the sheep repeatedly in the first indictment, indicating the tragic situation for the sheep. However, Zechariah prophesied that the good shepherd would be stricken, also resulting in the scattering of the sheep (Zech 13:7). As in the Gospel of John, so also

---

[17] Joachim Jeremias, "ποιμήν, […]" in *TDNT*, ed. Gerhard Kittel and Gerhard Friedrich, trans. Geoffrey W. Bromiley (Grand Rapids: Eerdmans, 1968), 6:488–89.

[18] Ibid., 496–97.

in the Gospel of Mark, Jesus takes up the metaphor of the shepherd as a means of describing His ministry. But here, He draws explicitly upon the prophecy of Zechariah 13 to explain the fulcrum of His ministry.

Unlike the divine judgment upon evil kings in Jeremiah and Ezekiel, the scattering of the sheep in both Zechariah and Mark is due to the vicarious death of the shepherd on behalf of the sheep. Mark 14:27–28 conveys the deeper meaning of the prophecy of Zechariah 13. There is a twofold movement here. In the first place, Jesus explains that all of the disciples are going to stumble—"because of Me this night, for it is written" (Mark 14:27). The death of their shepherd, Jesus emphasizes, is required by the text. Scripture must be fulfilled through the death of the "Shepherd" (Zech 13:7; Mark 14:27). However, the death of the Shepherd and the scattering of His sheep does not complete the fulfillment of prophecy.

In the second place, Zech 13:8–9 foretold that there must be a refining "through the fire" for the sheep. In particular, as a result of the refinement accomplished in the Shepherd's death, the Lord will declare a remnant of the sheep to be, "My people." The death of the Shepherd is a means of transformation for God to bring His flock into safety. Just as Mark 14:27 brought Zech 13:7 into the picture, Mark 14:28 then brought Zech 13:8–9 into the picture. First, through the death of the Shepherd the sheep are scattered and refined. But that is not the conclusion, for it is subsequently through the resurrection of the Shepherd, Jesus the Christ, that the scattered sheep will afterwards be gathered in Galilee (Mark 16:7; cp. Matt 18:16; John 21:1).

Jesus could thus summarize the whole purpose of His ministry: "for the Son of Man has come to seek and to save that which was lost" (Luke 19:10). The gospel of Jesus Christ, His vicarious death and victorious resurrection, was foretold in Zechariah's prophecy of the slain and risen Shepherd. The good Shepherd had a twofold ministry. First, the sheep had to be scattered in refinement through their Shepherd's death. Second, the sheep were then gathered in safety through their Shepherd's resurrection.[19]

---

[19] "The death of Jesus thus initiates the eschatological tribulation, the scattering and decimation of the flock, and the testing of the remnant that is left in the furnace. But the crisis, the scandal, is the turning point, for it is followed by the gathering of the purified

In the New Testament, the epicenter is not with Christian ministers as shepherds but with Christ as the Shepherd. Indeed, "Only once in the New Testament are congregational leaders called shepherds, namely, in the list of offices in Eph 4:11."[20] The verbal form of shepherding (Gk. *poimainein*) is used thrice to describe the responsibility of Christian ministers (1 Pet 5:2; Acts 20:28; John 21:16), and the noun for the flock (Gk. *poimnion*) is used to describe the Christian congregation.[21] But the emphasis is upon Christ Jesus as the Shepherd. The author of Hebrews identifies Jesus as "that great Shepherd of the sheep," who offered the blood of the eternal covenant through His death (Heb 13:20). Peter refers to Jesus as "the Chief Shepherd," who will hold the elders responsible for the flock that He entrusted to them (1 Pet 5:1–4). Jesus is clear that His role as Shepherd over the sheep is a universal one; He begins with the "fold" in Israel, but other sheep must be included and "there will be one flock and one shepherd" (John 10:16). The great Shepherd of the universal church is Christ Jesus alone.

Christ Jesus is universally present to the sheep as their Shepherd, and He is united inwardly with the sheep (John 10:14–15). Unlike the hireling shepherd, who might flee at the first sign of danger, Jesus lays down His life for His sheep (John 10:11–13). The heart of the Lord is clearly with His sheep. During His earthly ministry, the Gospel of Mark records that He saw the multitude and "was moved with compassion [Gk. *esplagchnisthē*] for them" (Mark 6:34). The use of *splagchnizomai* here indicates a deeply felt sympathy that is generated from love in the heart.[22] The heartfelt compassion of the Lord is entirely different from the cold indifference and even abusive intent displayed toward the sheep in Ezekiel's description of the shepherd-kings of Israel. Jesus is the good Shepherd who gathers the sheep, protects the sheep, and dies for the sheep. Jesus will also gather the sheep to Himself in the end of time in order to judge them righteously (Matt 25:31–32). Jesus will feed (Gk. *poimanei*) His sheep

---

flock as the people of God under the leadership of the Good Shepherd." Jeremias, in *TDNT*, "ποιμήν, [etc.]," 6:493 (see n. 17).

    20 Ibid., 6:497.
    21 Ibid., "ποίμνη, […]," 6:500–2.
    22 BAGD, s.v. "Σπλαγχνίζομαι," 762–63.

like only the great Shepherd can, for He is the Lord who has the heart of a sheep, too. He is the shepherd who truly understands and truly loves His sheep. He lived and died as the Lamb (Gk. *to arnion*), and He occupies the divine throne, from which He ministers peace and provision to His sheep (Rev 7:17).

The Evil Shepherds of Ezekiel 34:5–8

The dark depravity of the evil shepherds in Ezekiel 34 comes into especially sharp relief against the brilliant and beautiful light provided in the revelation of Jesus Christ as the good Shepherd. A look into the behavior of the evil shepherds will reinforce this reality. F. B. Huey argues that ancient shepherds had three primary responsibilities, all of which may be seen negatively in the early verses of Ezekiel 34. First, the shepherd must "provide food, water, and a resting place for the sheep."[23] But the shepherds of Israel were under judgment precisely because they were concerned about providing these things for themselves rather than for the sheep (Ezek 34:3). Second, shepherds "took care of the sick sheep, dressed their wounds, and hunted for sheep that strayed from the flock."[24] However, the shepherds of Israel were doing the exact opposite; they were abusive toward the flock (Ezek 34:4).

The third responsibility that the ancient shepherd had "was to protect the sheep from danger."[25] The shepherd held a staff that could either be used to ward off a dangerous animal or that could be used to retrieve a sheep that had fallen into a crevice or otherwise become trapped in the underbrush. In our focal passage, Ezek 34:5–8, is found the Lord's verdict regarding the neglect of the shepherds to protect the sheep:

> "So they were scattered because there was no shepherd; and they became food for all the beasts of the field when they were scattered. My sheep wandered through all the mountains, and on every

---

[23] F. B. Huey, Jr., *Ezekiel, Daniel*, Layman's Bible Book Commentary (Nashville: Broadman Press, 1983), 80.

[24] Ibid.

[25] Ibid.

high hill; yes, My flock was scattered over the face of the earth, and no one was seeking or searching for them."

Therefore, you shepherds, hear the word of the LORD: "As I live," says the Lord GOD, "surely because My flock became a prey, and My flock became food for every beast of the field, because there was no shepherd, nor did my shepherds search for My flock, but the shepherds fed themselves and did not feed My flock."

Jesus Christ's description of the hired shepherds, who neglected their office at the first sign of a dangerous wolf, similarly applies to these faithless shepherds of ancient Israel. Jesus identified the "hireling" as one who does not really deserve the name of shepherd. The hireling does not care for the sheep, for he has no sense of ownership (John 10:12–13). The comparison is appropriate for the situation of Ezekiel. The last kings of Judah, who followed one another in rapid succession in the final years of the kingdom, did not really care about the flock of the Lord. They did not even search for the sheep that had been deported from the land into Babylon, much less risk their lives to redeem the flock (as Jesus would one day do). The neglect of the shepherds meant that the sheep were scattered and had become prey for the beasts of the field.

John Taylor and Leslie Allen agree that the kings of Israel were given responsibility for the dangerous plight of the people as refugees. "Instead of keeping the flock together in safety they allowed them to be scattered over all the earth. . . . This meant that they were an easy prey for wild beasts, representing here the hostile nations of the world."[26] "Responsibility for the deportation of 597 BC and for the flight of refugees from Judah to neighboring states is laid at the palace door."[27] The word *puts*, which is translated as "scattered," is used thrice in this passage. Sheep are at their most vulnerable when they are separated from one another and from their shepherd. One of the ancient shepherd's primary responsibilities was to keep the sheep together in his presence. When the shepherd does not tend to the sheep and gather them regularly into the fold, they will naturally

---

[26] John B. Taylor, *Ezekiel: An Introduction and Commentary*, Tyndale Old Testament Commentaries (Downers Grove, IL: InterVarsity Press, 1969), 220.
[27] Allen, *Ezekiel 20–48*, 161.

"wander" (Hb. *shagah*). It is in such a state of dispersion that a flock becomes a series of individuals, who then make easy "prey" (*baz*). In a horrifying figure of speech evocative of cannibalism, Ezekiel points out that the people as sheep thereby become "food" or "meat" (Hb. *'oklah*) for the conqueror as "beast" or "wild animal" (Hb. *chay*).

The issue is then raised, "Why did the shepherds allow the sheep to be scattered?" Ezekiel also provides the answer to that important question. A shepherd's constant task in his role of protecting the flock was to "seek" (Hb. *baqash*) and "search" (Hb. *darash*) for the sheep, monitoring them to keep them from endangering themselves or to remove them from the peril of predators. When a shepherd is not monitoring the sheep in this fashion, they will easily become scattered and endangered. Rather than being focused on tending the flock, however, Israel's shepherds were focused on tending themselves ("but the shepherds fed themselves and did not feed My flock," Ezek 34:8).

These verses from Ezekiel 34 present a very dark picture, but the passage is not without indications of hope. Repeatedly, the Lord refers in this passage to the people as "My sheep" or "My flock" (vv. 6, 8). The kings as shepherds may act as hirelings, but there is a Shepherd who owns this flock, who has a vested and intimate interest in the welfare of his sheep. Israel and Judah may have had various kings who were to function as shepherds, but they also have their covenant Lord God, who is ultimately the King whom they must worship (cp. Ps 98:6) and ultimately the Shepherd who will rescue them (Ezek 34:11–16, 20–31). And in a rich allusion to the Messiah who would be their only Shepherd, the Lord also promises, "I will establish one shepherd over them, and he shall feed them—My servant David. He shall feed them and be their shepherd. And I, the LORD, will be their God, and My servant David a prince among them" (Ezek 34:23–24a). Israel's motley crew of faithless and vanquished shepherd-kings would be replaced with a singularly faithful and victorious Shepherd-King, the Christ. The Lord's promise regarding the Davidic "one shepherd" (Ezek 34:23), within the overarching context of the Lord's promise to act decisively as Israel's Shepherd (Ezek 34:20–31), brings the human Messiah and the Lord God into a profound unity redolent of the New Testament's high Christology.

The Rod and the Staff: The Christian
Office of the Shepherd Theologian

Only in light of the great Shepherd, Jesus Christ, discussed above, should the ministry of those who may be appropriately entitled "under-shepherds" be perceived. "Pastors," also known as "elders" and "over-seers," hold a very important office in the New Testament churches, but it is an entirely derivative and ultimately responsible office. The English word "pastor" derives from the Latin *pascere*, which indicates foraging or grazing. Its most literal meaning is "shepherd." One of the shepherd's primary roles is that of being the congregation's official teacher or theologian. As the flock feeds on the Word of God while it grazes in the world, the shepherd-theologian ensures that verdant fields are available to his congregation and that dangers are avoided.

On what basis is there correlation between the pastor and the theologian? Alas, the academic theologian and the church pastor have developed historically into separate offices,[28] but this was not always the case. Paul's description of the church office of the "pastor" is intentionally coupled with the description of his office as a "teacher" of the gospel of Jesus Christ (Eph 4:11). In Ephesians 4, among the gifts that the ascended Lord gave to the church were the two "foundation" offices of the apostles and prophets.[29] The third office, the "evangelist," is to proclaim the gospel to unbelievers for the sake of converting them. The fourth office is given a twofold description—"pastors and teachers." In coupling the metaphor of shepherding with the role of teaching, Paul may have been reflecting upon the Lord's promise, "And I will give you shepherds according to My heart, who will feed you with knowledge and understanding" (Jer 3:15).

After new believers have been incorporated into the church, they require continual instruction by their pastor-teachers or shepherd-theologians.

---

[28] Owen Strachan, "Of Scholars and Saints: A Brief History of the Pastorate," in Kevin J. Vanhoozer and Owen Strachan, *The Pastor as Public Theologian: Reclaiming a Lost Vision* (Grand Rapids: Baker, 2015), 69–93. I would emphasize that every Christian is a theologian, even as the pastor(s) hold(s) the primary office of theologian within the congregation.

[29] F. F. Bruce, *The Epistles to the Colossians, to Philemon, and to the Ephesians*, NICNT (Grand Rapids: Eerdmans, 1984), 303–6, 346.

F. F. Bruce argues, "Teaching is an essential part of the pastoral ministry; it is appropriate, therefore, that the two terms, 'pastors and teachers,' should be joined together to denote one order of ministry."[30] In effect, the Christian pastor has the incredible power of the Word of God to wield, and to that Word he must be carefully bound. Through the proclamation of the Word of God to the people of God, the Christian leader fulfills his role as a shepherd, and the congregation to which he is temporally responsible will recognize his authority only in that Word.[31] The Christian shepherd's role may be summarized as that of caring for the congregation (Acts 20:28; 1 Pet 5:2–4), seeking the little ones who have become lost (Matt 18:10–14), and combatting heretical teachings in the flock (Acts 20:29–30). In each of these three metaphorical cases, from feeding to finding to fighting, the shepherd operates literally through teaching a theological message from the Word of God. The Word of God can be described as working through the correction of the law and the healing of the gospel, by which sheep may grow healthy and strong (cp. Heb 5:12–6:3). It should go without saying that the role of the shepherd-theologian is not for him to fulfill the ministry of the church but for him to equip the people to fulfill the ministry of the church (Eph 4:12).

The shepherd's task of finding or seeking out those sheep that have wandered away is particularly emphasized in the New Testament. Jesus lauded the praiseworthiness of searching for the lost sheep (Luke 15:4) as strongly as Ezekiel condemned the evil shepherds for neglecting the same (Ezek 34:5–8). Two major causes for the wandering of the sheep into danger are doctrinal and moral. The moral cause is seen in the wayward heart, whose greed causes a person to "pierce" himself "with many sorrows" (1 Tim 6:10). The doctrinal cause for wandering is seen in the fascination of some people for "profane and idle babblings and contradictions of what is falsely called knowledge" (1 Tim 6:20–21). A shepherd-theologian brings back those who have wandered into theological error and moral travesty by presenting the "fire" of the law and the "mercy" of the gospel

---

[30] Ibid., 348.

[31] Cp. Malcolm B. Yarnell III, "The Church," in *The Baptist Faith and Message 2000: Critical Issues in America's Largest Protestant Denomination*, ed. Douglas K. Blount and Joseph D. Wooddell (New York: Rowman & Littlefield, 2007), 62–63.

(Jude 22–23). The shepherd's ministry of rescuing the wandering is one of great joy, for he is saving souls (Jas 5:19–20) and restoring them to a right relationship with the great Shepherd (1 Pet 2:25).

Finally, let it be noted that God will hold the Christian undershepherd accountable for how he conducts himself in his office. Christ modeled the perfect attitude for His shepherd-theologians. Like Christ, we[32] must lead His flock out to witness in the culture, but then we must lead them back into worship and protect them while they rest (John 10:1–5).[33] And in the fold, the shepherd must function as a doorkeeper, who is keen to guard against wolves, even at cost to his own life (John 10:7–15).[34] Wolves are difficult to identify and aggressive when cornered, but they may be known through their words and actions (Matt 7:15–16; Acts 20:29). Because of the deceptiveness and destructiveness of the wolves, being a shepherd is difficult and dangerous work. Jesus said that it requires the development of the wisdom of a serpent balanced with the moral innocence of a dove (Matt 10:16).

New Testament church leaders, therefore, must be extremely careful that their hearts are focused on Christ and their actions on their flock. Shepherd-theologians should not be like the wicked Israelite king-shepherds, who were focused on "feeding themselves" (Gk. *heautous poi-mainontes*, Jude 12). Sadly, there are too many cases where contemporary pastors neglect the flocks that the Lord placed in their care and pursue their own self-interests instead. The shepherd who has descended into ministry for money and not for love has become a despicable hireling. However, if a pastor-theologian discovers his heart's intentions toward God and his outward actions toward the flock have been engrossed with evil, he need not utterly despair. For the errant shepherd-theologian who has neglected

---

[32] For reasons to include some academic theologians in the pastorate, see Malcolm B. Yarnell III, "To the End of Glorifying Jesus: The Scholar's Calling to the Churches," *Faith & Mission* 19 (2001): 25–32.

[33] The imagery is one of the shepherd "leading" sheep that "follow" him, rather than of a shepherd "driving" the sheep forcefully before him. Leon Morris, *The Gospel According to John*, revised ed., NICNT (Grand Rapids: Eerdmans, 1995), 447.

[34] While Christ is the only One who dies for the salvation of the sheep and is thus the only door to eternal life, the undershepherd may function as a doorkeeper. On the role of the doorkeeper in relation to the shepherd, see Morris, *The Gospel According to John*, 446–47.

his flock and heedlessly allowed them to wander morally and doctrinally, there is yet hope for repentance and restoration.

The first pastor to be instituted was Peter, and in spite of his claims that he loved Christ more than any of the other disciples did (Mark 14:29), he failed. Not once nor twice but thrice Peter denied Jesus in His greatest hour of human need (Mark 14:66–72; John 18:15–18, 25–27). But in a moving redemptive moment for Peter and potentially for every shepherd-theologian since Peter, the Lord recommissioned His fallen undershepherd (John 21:15–17).[35] The risen Christ thrice correlated Peter's love for the Lord with Peter's fulfillment of his appointed office to shepherd the flock. Only when Peter fully embraced the cross of the shepherding office Christ had given him did Peter find that his heart was truly following his Lord (John 21:18–19).

The only way a Christian undershepherd may avoid becoming an evil shepherd like those in judgment under Ezekiel is through a heart continually transformed by the Word of God and the Spirit of God to take the shape of the cross of the Lord Jesus Christ, who is primarily concerned for His flock's welfare and seeks them out to save them. May we, Christ's shepherd-theologians, have self-sacrificial ministries that follow the good Shepherd of the New Testament rather than the self-centered actions of the evil shepherds indicted in Ezekiel.

---

[35] "There can be little doubt but that the whole scene is meant to show us Peter as completely restored to his position of leadership" (Ibid., 772).

CHAPTER 7

Bring Back Those Driven Away

Tommy Kiker

O n the highways of North Texas there are many electronic signs disseminating information to travelers. Among the notifications on those signs are Amber Alerts, letting you know there is a missing or abducted child. There are even times when phones give out a loud alert as well. Do you look at these and consider that particular family's situation, or do you just ignore it and get irritated that your phone is making so much noise? What if that sign or notification was alerting the masses about *your* child missing? That would dramatically change your response. It would change everything. I pray that no one reading this book ever has to experience that crisis, but this example gives insight into the kind of shepherd who pleases the Lord. The greater the love a shepherd has for the sheep who are in his charge, the more diligence he takes in their care.

The shepherd who pleases the Lord has a genuine love and concern for the sheep, works diligently to keep them from being scattered, and searches diligently for them when they are out of the fold. What are the responsibilities and expectations of a worthy shepherd in the area of bringing back the scattered? What can be gleaned from Ezekiel 34 and other portions of Scripture to define the role of the minister as a shepherd? Answers are found by examining the passages and understanding how they can be applied today.

Implications of Ezekiel 34

Ezekiel prophesied during an incredibly difficult time for the nation of Judah. The people were in the midst of God's judgment, which resulted in their exile and the ultimate destruction of the temple and the city of Jerusalem. The events that occurred were God's judgment of His people's continual disobedience and failure to listen to the prophets, who declared to them the Word of the Lord.

The call of Ezekiel in chapters 1–3 and his vision of the dry bones coming back to life in chapter 37 are perhaps the more well-known events of the prophet's writings. However, Scripture reveals one of the clearer pictures of the shepherd in Ezekiel 34 where the Lord contrasts the shepherds who had failed in their assignment with a climactic picture of the ideal shepherd.

Ezekiel declared God's prophecy against the shepherds of Israel. These shepherds were the religious and political leaders of God's nation, who had failed to lead Israel in a way that consistently honored God. The books of Kings and Chronicles reveal that this failure to heed the Lord's commands had been a perennial failure on the part of the leaders of Israel and Judah. God's judgment was inevitable. The words of God against the shepherds of Israel reveal several areas where worthy shepherds should give attention. God shows these areas through the shepherds' failures.

As earlier chapters have already discussed, the shepherds failed in their responsibilities to feed the flock, strengthen the weak, heal the sick, bind up the broken, and protect the flock. Subsequent chapters of this work will demonstrate how they were also accountable for failing to seek the lost and lead the flock.

The focus of this chapter is on the shepherds' failure to bring back those sheep that were driven away. God called Ezekiel to prophesy against the shepherds because they had not "brought back what was driven away, nor sought what was lost" (v. 4). Not only had they not brought them back, but they were not even seeking those that were scattered. Verse 6 reiterates,

"My flock was scattered over the whole face of the earth, and no one was seeking or searching for them." The shepherds were responsible for the scattering of the sheep in the first place because of their failure to feed, protect, and care for the flock. Once they were scattered, the shepherds could not be bothered even to look for the straying sheep. When Ezekiel describes God as Shepherd later in the chapter, he puts a distinct emphasis on the importance of seeking out and bringing back the scattered.

The numerous failures of the shepherds demanded God's judgment upon them. In Ezekiel 34:7–10 is God's declaration. God called on them twice in the four short verses to "hear the Word of the Lord." He declared their failures to feed, protect, heal, mend, and tend the flock. He also condemned their lack of concern for the sheep's well-being, even after they had been scattered. For these reasons, the Lord declared that He is against the shepherds, that they are to give an account for the sheep, and He chastises them for their failure to bring the sheep back. Ultimately, God declared that He would deliver the sheep from their hands.

There are many implications for ministers today to be gleaned from God's indictment of the shepherds in Ezekiel 34. The primary purpose of this chapter is to consider the process of *bringing back those driven away*. The chapter will begin by addressing why sheep scatter. Next, it will focus on the work of the good Shepherd toward sheep who have been scattered and driven away. Finally, steps to be taken that the sheep may not be scattered will be addressed, as well as how shepherds should go about bringing them back if and when they are "driven away."

Understand Why Sheep May Scatter

The imagery in Ezekiel 34 reveals why sheep may scatter. They go out searching for food when they are unfed. Sheep scatter when there is no shepherd to warn or fight off the prey seeking to devour them. Zechariah declared the responsibility of the shepherds and the results of their being derelict of duty: "Therefore the people wend their way like sheep; / They are in trouble because there is no shepherd. / My anger is kindled against the shepherds, / And I will punish the goatherds" (Zech 10:2–3).

Jeremiah, relaying the word of the Lord, also explained the responsibility of the shepherds in the scattering of the Lord's flock:

> My people have been lost sheep.
> Their shepherds have led them astray;
> They have turned them away on the mountains.
> They have gone from mountain to hill;
> They have forgotten their resting place. (Jer 50:6)

The shepherds of Israel had failed to heed the warnings of God, and God let pagan nations conquer and scatter His people. Thus, Jeremiah lamented:

> Israel is like scattered sheep;
> The lions have driven him away.
> First the king of Assyria devoured him;
> Now at last this Nebuchadnezzar king of Babylon has broken his bones. (Jer 50:17)

Sheep, when left unattended, tend to stray as Isaiah 53:6 describes, "All we like sheep have gone astray; / We have turned, every one, to his own way." God takes very seriously the care of His sheep and declares His judgment on irresponsible and unworthy shepherds. He declared:

> "For the shepherds have become dull-hearted,
> And have not sought the LORD;
> Therefore they shall not prosper,
> And all their flocks shall be scattered." (Jer 10:21)

Later, the Lord, again through Jeremiah, warned of the consequences of the failure of the shepherds:

> And the shepherds will have no way to flee,
> Nor the leaders of the flock to escape.
> A voice of the cry of the shepherds,
> And a wailing of the leaders to the flock will be heard.
> For the LORD has plundered their pasture,
> And the peaceful dwellings are cut down

Because of the fierce anger of the LORD.
He has left His lair like the lion;
For their land is desolate
Because of the fierceness of the Oppressor,
And because of His fierce anger. (Jer 25:35–38)

Sheep in the church tend to scatter because there is a real enemy who desires to destroy the children of God. Jesus highlighted this reality when He commissioned the disciples to go out into the world. He warned them, "Behold, I send you out as sheep in the midst of wolves. Therefore be wise as serpents and harmless as doves" (Matt 10:16). Sheep need to know the dangers that they face, and one of the responsibilities of a worthy shepherd is to alert them. The shepherd should provide warning and protection from the evils of this world and offer hope and healing when sheep are harmed because of their sin or the sin of others. A shepherd must be diligent to be at his post and not abandon the sheep.

Ultimately, every child of God will give an account for his own decisions. However, Scripture makes clear that those placed in positions of leadership with and over the sheep hold a great level of responsibility and will be held accountable. The negative example of the shepherds in Ezekiel 34 is a warning on how not to be a shepherd, but the chapter also contrasts what a good shepherd does as it points to the example of the Lord.

The Example of the Good Shepherd

The most magnificent shepherd imagery in Scripture applies to God. Psalm 23 is probably the most often quoted Old Testament text that pictures the Lord as a Shepherd. The beloved psalm shows that the good Shepherd offers provision ("makes me to lie down in green pastures; / He leads me beside still waters," v. 2), protection ("Your rod and Your staff, they comfort me," v. 4), and promise ("Surely goodness and mercy shall follow me / All the days of my life," v. 6).

In Ezekiel 34, God declares that He will search for the sheep and seek them out (v. 11). God determines to do what the shepherds had failed to do (i.e., seek and bring back those that had been scattered). God promises to feed His flock, seek what is lost, bring back what is driven away, bind up the broken, and strengthen the sick (vv. 14–16). God also introduces a coming judgment for those sheep who were not genuine and had not faithfully followed His direction. Despite the poor leadership of the shepherds, the sheep are not without responsibility.

Clearly the appointed shepherds had failed in their expected responsibilities. On one hand, their poor example serves as an exhortation and a warning for the pastor not to take lightly the responsibilities of the shepherd. On the other hand, God's example encourages pastors to take seriously that which God takes seriously—His sheep. The mandate to bring back lost sheep is vividly pictured in this chapter.

Numerous references in Ezekiel 34 point to God's clear concern and compassion for His people. A summary of these references helps to highlight the heart of God concerning the sheep that have been scattered. "For thus says the Lord GOD: 'Indeed I Myself will *search* for My sheep and *seek* them out'" (v. 11).[1] Two words in the same sentence describe the actions of a good shepherd: "search" and "seek." The language of seeking continues in verse 12, but a determination to deliver them from their condition is added: "As a shepherd *seeks* out his flock . . . so I will *seek* out My sheep and *deliver* them from all the places where they were scattered" (v. 12). In the next verse the same language appears again: "I will *bring them out* from the peoples and *gather* them . . . and will *bring them to* their own land" (v. 13).

The ultimate goal of searching and seeking is to bring the sheep back to the fold. The words are repeated later in the text when God reiterates, "I will *seek* what was lost and *bring back* what was driven away" (v. 16). Similar language portraying the protection that a faithful shepherd brings is introduced as well. A shepherd who genuinely seeks after the scattered to bring them back benefits the sheep by helping them find the added protection of the flock and the shepherds. God declares, "I will save My flock, and they shall no longer be prey . . . I will . . . cause wild beasts to cease from the land . . . and they [My sheep] shall no longer be prey for the nations" (vv. 22, 25, 28).

---

[1] All italics in the quoted verses have been added for emphasis.

In Ezek 34:23, the reader is introduced to another shepherd. God announces, "I will establish one shepherd over them, and he shall feed them—My servant David. He shall feed them and be their shepherd." This shepherd is Jesus. God presents Himself as the faithful Shepherd to His nation Israel, and Jesus was foretold as the coming Shepherd for all people. The chapter concludes with several contrasts between the faithful Shepherd's care for the sheep and the self-indulgent negligence of the unfaithful shepherds condemned in the first part of the chapter.

God exemplifies the faithful shepherd, because only a true shepherd genuinely cares for the sheep. Even in the midst of the judgment found in the book of Ezekiel—the exile and destruction of Jerusalem—God, the good Shepherd, gives hope and assurance of a coming restoration. The people of God, from their leaders down, had rebelled and consistently disobeyed God, but God in His grace proclaims His promise. They are His sheep and He is their God. "'You are My flock, the flock of My pasture; you are men, and I am your God,' says the Lord GoD" (v. 31).

The shepherd imagery extends to the New Testament with many passages providing further insight into the responsibility of the shepherd toward the sheep who are driven away. In the book of Acts, Paul used the shepherd motif when he gave parting instructions to the elders. Paul exhorted the elders to "take heed to yourselves and to all the flock, among which the Holy Spirit has made you overseers, to shepherd the church of God which He purchased with His own blood" (Acts 20:28). Paul continued with the picture of wolves and those who would try to attack the sheep. The shepherd exists to protect the sheep by preventing them from being scattered.

Peter also employs the shepherd image. He explains that the pastor should serve with a shepherd's mindset always pointing his sheep to the Chief Shepherd:

Shepherd the flock of God which is among you, serving as overseers, not by compulsion but willingly, not for dishonest gain but eagerly; nor as being lords over those entrusted to you, but being examples to the flock; and when the Chief Shepherd appears, you will receive the crown of glory that does not fade away. (1 Pet 5:2–4)

Peter also introduces the protection function when he reminds the elders to "be sober, be vigilant; because your adversary the devil walks about like a roaring lion, seeking whom he may devour" (1 Pet 5:8).

The clearest picture of the role of the shepherd is seen in Jesus. Often the New Testament reveals the heart of Jesus as the Shepherd toward those who were driven away. Even the prophecy of His birth portrays such a picture. The religious leaders in Jerusalem knew the prophecy fulfilled by Jesus's birth in Bethlehem: "For out of you [Bethlehem] shall come a Ruler / Who will shepherd My people Israel" (Matt 2:6; Mic 5:2). The genuine compassion of Jesus is seen throughout the Gospels. Jesus saw the people as sheep who were weary, scattered, and without a shepherd (Matt 9:36). He also presented a clear mandate of the importance of bringing back those who are scattered in the parable of the Lost Sheep in Luke 15 and Matthew 18. Peter saw Jesus as "the Chief Shepherd" (1 Pet 5:4) and as "the Shepherd and Overseer" of our souls (1 Pet 2:25). The author of Hebrews declared that Jesus is the "great Shepherd of the sheep" through His "blood of the everlasting covenant" (Heb 13:20). Finally, John, in a crescendo of praise, declared his vision of the Lamb who "will shepherd them and lead them to living fountains of waters. And God will wipe away every tear from their eyes" (Rev 7:17).

The responsibility of the shepherd to sheep who have been driven away is also clearly revealed in John 10. In this chapter, rich with shepherd language, Jesus declared that He is "the Good Shepherd, and that a good shepherd gives his life for the sheep." The example for pastors who desire to be true shepherds is established by Jesus. One can only serve as a faithful shepherd when he is willing to lay down his life for the sheep—certainly not in the same way that Jesus did, but out of a genuine love and concern for the spiritual welfare of the people.

Jesus described the unfaithful shepherd as "a hireling." One who does not know or genuinely care for the sheep sees the danger coming and leaves the sheep to fend for themselves. Such actions cause the sheep to be harmed and scattered. Why does a hireling do this? Because he does not care for the sheep!

This is precisely the problem God was addressing in Ezekiel 34, and it is all too relevant today. Too many shepherds are motivated by their own desires, greed, and self-promotion; they have no real genuine concern for the sheep. A good shepherd, a faithful shepherd, a God-honoring pastor has a willingness to lay down his life, his goals, and his comfort for the sheep. Such a genuine love is the key for keeping the sheep from being scattered and the passion that drives a faithful shepherd to seek them when they are scattered and bring them back.

General Principles for Bringing Back the Sheep and Preventing Others from Being Scattered

A shepherd who has a genuine love and concern for the spiritual welfare of the sheep serves with much greater effectiveness. The reality is that even with a genuine love for the congregation, a pastor often finds it difficult to keep the sheep from straying and even more difficult to bring them back effectively when they do scatter. There are four general principles every church and pastor should consider to bring back those driven away and prevent more from straying: (1) faithful evangelism, (2) meaningful membership, (3) lifelong discipleship, and (4) corrective and restorative church discipline.

Faithful Evangelism

Remember to draw them with what you will have to keep them. Many churches are more concerned about drawing a crowd than seeking and recovering lost sheep. "Members" come and go because they had some peripheral need met or were attracted to a particular element of the church but never had a genuine conversion experience. As shepherds and as the body of Christ, we must be diligent to present unashamedly the simple yet profound gospel message. Paul reminds us "that Christ died for our sins, according to the Scriptures, and that He was buried, and that He rose again the third day according to the Scriptures" (1 Cor 15:3–4).

Meaningful Membership

In many ways more commitment is required to join a local wholesale discount club than to join or leave the membership of churches in America.

A consumer-driven culture has caused many to view church as a place that serves them rather than Christ. The "one another" statements throughout Scripture make for a wonderful study and give a beautiful picture of how the body should love and serve one another.[2]

Meaningful church membership should include a concerted effort to maintain a regenerate church membership, meaning that as far as we are able to know, the membership is composed of genuine believers. The practice of clearly presenting and explaining the gospel, as mentioned previously, plays an important role in this process, but the examination of those who are already members is important as well.

A pastor has no greater opportunity to examine the spiritual genuineness of the membership than when he first comes on the field. I would implore every pastor to take the time and energy to hear the personal testimony of each member of the church he serves. To sit with church members, get to know them, and learn how they came to know Jesus is a sweet visit to make. It often provides opportunity to give clarity or to help some recognize that they have never truly surrendered to Christ. In a larger church, this task would need to be shared, but steps are easily taken to have such opportunities going forward. Many scatter from the flock because they never really became a part of it in the first place.

Lifelong Discipleship

The church is called to make disciples. How long does this process last? I am convinced that proper evangelism, followed by meaningful membership and a lifetime discipleship process is most effective in building a healthy church. There must be intentionality in our churches to develop a ministry of discipleship that is more than just programs. A plethora

---

[2] Numerous passages in Scripture use "one another" language to describe the relationship in the body of Christ. One prominent example is found in Romans 12, where Paul reminds the church at Rome that they are "members of one another" (v. 5), they are to give "preference to one another" (v. 10), and they are to have the "same mind toward one another" (v. 16). Other references include: 1 Cor 11:33; 12:25; Gal 5:13; 6:2; Eph 4:2, 25, 32; 5:19; Col 3:13, 16; 1 Thess 3:12; 4:9, 18; 5:11; Heb 10:24–25; Jas 4:11; 5:9, 16; 1 Pet 1:22; 3:8; 4:8–10; 5:5; 1 John 1:7; 3:11.

of programs is available, and many churches use numbers of them, but what is the end goal? What is the plan?

Some churches seem to throw programs out there, hoping that something works, rather than developing a plan that fits the place and people who are being served. There certainly are elements of any discipleship plan that should be included in every church, but the process by which these elements are accomplished is unique to each church. We must not neglect the labor of diligently seeking God and His wisdom rather than just repackaging what seems to be working other places.

Every discipleship plan should provide members multiple connections to the body as a whole. These connections need to include family discipleship and small-group interaction as well as large-group opportunities. There should be a clear path laid out and measurable goals for the individual, the family, and the church. The end result should be providing the resources necessary to help develop mature believers who are faithfully involved in ministry.

Corrective and Restorative Church Discipline

The first three principles have a preventive focus. The establishment of a clear understanding of the gospel, meaningful membership, and a lifetime plan of discipleship lay a foundation that aids individuals in remaining strongly connected to the body. Even with such a foundation, the church currently exists in a fallen world, and genuine believers are not immune from the destruction of sin. A final principle used to bring back those who have been driven away is biblical church discipline.

If church discipline is to be effective there must be meaningful membership and an agreement or covenant among church members that they commit to bring themselves under such loving care. If there is no such understanding and consistent teaching, then church discipline is seen only as judgmental and destructive. For a church body that takes seriously the gospel, including church membership and the growth of each individual member, church discipline is a loving and powerful gift. Church discipline is often viewed, even by many who practice it, as a step to be taken in the most grievous of situations.

Church discipline would be more effective if it were to begin in simple areas such as attendance and faithfulness to expectations of church members. If the church truly loves and serves one another, the members would be much more diligent to speak into situations long before they reach life-shattering levels such as adultery or divorce. What if shepherds cared so much about the sheep and the members cared so much about each other that even the hint of such things were quickly addressed in a loving and restorative way? What if it became nearly impossible for someone to drift away from the body because there were too many parts of the body who genuinely cared for that person and who would be diligent lovingly to speak truth into the situation? This commitment is possible, not in our flesh or in our strength but only in the power of the Holy Spirit. With the heart of Christ, the body of Christ would constantly practice discipline in a way that heals rather than destroys and that brings back—instead of driving further away—those who have scattered.[3]

The Rod and the Staff: Bringing Sheep Back to the Flock

The understanding of the biblical material concerning the shepherd's responsibility for bringing back those who have been driven away is not incredibly difficult to understand. The actual process of preventing the sheep from being scattered and bringing them back when they do scatter is much more difficult. The following are practical implications that I pray burn in your heart every day of your ministry. A good shepherd faithfully shows up and personally knows his sheep. By these simple steps we are driven to grow in our knowledge of the sheep and in a genuine, Christlike love for the sheep, which enables us by the power of the Spirit to stay focused on the task.

---

[3] The following works provide a helpful introduction to the topics of meaningful church membership, church discipline, and other areas to be considered for the well-being of local churches. Thomas White, Jason G. Duesing, and Malcolm B. Yarnell III, eds., *Restoring Integrity in Baptist Churches* (Grand Rapids: Kregel, 2008); John S. Hammett and Benjamin Merkle, eds., *Those Who Must Give an Account: A Study of Church Membership and Church Discipline* (Nashville: B&H, 2012); Mark Dever and Jonathan Leeman, eds., *Baptist Foundations: Church Government for an Anti-Institutional Age* (Nashville: B&H, 2015).

Inaction Is Not Acceptable: Show Up

Pastors have a responsibility to the sheep. They cannot neglect nor abandon their posts without consequences to the sheep and to themselves. Scripture is clear that those who hold the office of pastor should be called, qualified; and certainly they should give an account of how they lead and tend the sheep of God. The pictures of shepherding in the Old Testament give clear warning to the responsibility of one entrusted with the care of God's sheep. There is no place for selfish shepherds. Clearly God was displeased with the shepherds described by Isaiah:

> Yes, they are greedy dogs
> Which never have enough.
> And they are shepherds
> Who cannot understand;
> They all look to their own way,
> Every one for his own gain,
> From his own territory. (Isa 56:11)

Such neglect and selfishness leads to the scattering of the sheep, and there are great consequences for this result.

Jeremiah delivered God's stern warning to such shepherds: "'Woe to the shepherds who destroy and scatter the sheep of My pasture!' says the LORD" (Jer 23:1). The prophet Zechariah delivered a similar warning from the Lord:

> Woe to the worthless shepherd,
> Who leaves the flock!
> A sword shall be against his arm
> And against his right eye;
> His arm shall completely wither,
> And his right eye shall be totally blinded. (Zech 11:17)

Clearly those entrusted with responsibility over God's flock were and are accountable before the God who has entrusted them with the care of His sheep.

The New Testament also warns against faithless shepherds. The writer of Hebrews declares, "Obey those who rule over you, and be submissive, for they watch out for your souls, as those who must give account" (13:17). James explains that teachers face "a stricter judgment" (3:1). With this understanding, pastors take on the great responsibility of tending the sheep; they must give an account, and they will face a stricter judgment.

The shepherds in Ezekiel 34 are charged with consistent neglect and even abandonment of their assigned duties. Much of what is necessary to perform the role of pastor/shepherd pertains to just showing up. The pastor preaches and teaches week by week, month by month, and year by year. The diet of consistent, faithful, accurate, and patient teaching of the truths of God's word is to be commended. However, very little of what the pastor says in his sermons is remembered even hours after they are delivered; but his presence in the time of joy, in the time of trial, and in the major spiritual moments of life is remembered for a lifetime.

Many times the pastor does not know what to say, and a relevant Scripture verse is certainly appropriate; but often the best course of action includes just being with the sheep. Share a quick verse of Scripture, voice a prayer of trust and petition to the Lord Jesus, but be present with the sheep. Be found present in the field with the sheep; then, when the enemy comes and tries to destroy and devour, the sheep trust that their shepherd is there to protect them.

Know the Sheep

Some shepherds, who have been called and appointed by God to tend to the sheep of a particular flock, do not even know who the sheep are or where many of them are located. One of the charges brought against the shepherds in Ezekiel 34 was that the sheep had been scattered, and the shepherds were not even searching for them. The first step shepherds must take to fulfill their tasks is to identify the sheep. Jesus said, "My sheep hear My voice, and I know them" (John 10:27). A shepherd cannot even know that a particular sheep is missing if he does not know who the sheep are in the first place.

Many churches (nearly all to which I have belonged in my life and ministry) need to search through the roll of their members and come to a reality of how many members they actually have. I have personally seen numerous church rolls that are bloated because of poor record keeping. Failure to record transfers and deaths leads to church rolls with hundreds or even thousands of names that cannot be identified or located.

One of the primary goals of any shepherd should be to have an accurate account of the sheep. There is nothing glamourous about being the clerk in a local church. However, there needs to be renewed recognition of how important this particular job is to the health and well-being of the local body of Christ. What are the main responsibilities of a church clerk or whatever person or committee is charged with the upkeep of an accurate church roll?

A current list of all church members with their contact information— including address, phone number, and email address—is vital. This information should normally be kept by family units, making it easier to keep track of members who belong to the same immediate family. The information should also contain important dates such as the member's birthday, anniversary, baptism, church membership, and current membership status. This type of information helps provide opportunities for ministry.

Once a pastor comes to a new field of ministry, he should begin diligently getting to know his sheep. There should be a genuine effort to use the church roll to contact every member and determine his current relationship with the church. In most situations this is a task too large for one individual, so the pastor should enlist other ministers, deacons, and key church leaders to help. I would not suggest calling this a "cleansing of the roll" or any type of church discipline at this point. The activity merely reflects a shepherd's genuine desire to know the identity of his sheep.

If my personal history is any guide, this type of investigation of the church roll reveals several different situations:

- A large number of church members are *consistently active*, and it is easy to update their information. The contacts the pastor makes with these individuals gives him opportunity to get to know them, their families, and their conversion testimonies. This interaction helps build relationships between the shepherd and his sheep.

- There are a good number of church members whose *attendance and involvement have declined.* A call or visit from the pastor or another church member goes a long way in reconnecting them to the body.
- The review of a church roll also turns up members who *have joined other churches* or no longer desire to be a part of that particular church family.
- Others *have gone on to eternity* and can easily be removed from the roll to give a more accurate account of the sheep.
- The roll likely lists as members several *people whom no one can identify or locate.* The church should make every effort to locate these individuals by enlisting the help of the entire body. If the church is unable to identify and locate the individuals, their names should be removed from the official church roll, but their information should be maintained in case of future opportunity to reach out to them.

Another helpful tool that can benefit pastors and the entire congregation is a current church pictorial and member directory. There is much more to knowing the sheep than having an accurate record of their names and contact information. A pictorial directory makes it much easier for the congregation to know each other by name and to pray for one another. A pastor should pray daily over the sheep, looking at their faces and reminding himself of the needs of the family. He should also teach the congregation to do the same. In the past, churches have had to hire an outside company to make such directories; but with advances in technology and software, nearly every church body includes someone who can make this a ministry in itself.[4] Initially the task may seem daunting; but once the roll has been updated, a directory can be produced and maintained without great difficulty but with potential for being a great blessing to the body.

Once a church has an accurate record of the sheep, diligence should be given to maintain the records accurately until Jesus returns. The accurate keeping of the church roll helps the shepherd keep sheep from scattering

---

[4] There are numerous examples of software that help churches manage their membership and offer a method of producing an online pictorial directory as one of the functions. The three that came most recommended to me at the time of this writing were: Church Office Online (www.churchofficeonline.com), Church Community Builder (www.church communitybuilder.com), and ChurchTrac Online (www.churchtraconline.com).

and lets him know if and when they do begin to drift away. Again, this task can be overwhelming for one individual, so a faithful shepherd establishes a system that makes sure each sheep and his family have the care needed. At the very least, if sheep begin drifting away, steps can be taken to minister in those situations.

The faithful shepherd knows the sheep and has a genuine love for the sheep. The faithful shepherd feeds the sheep and has a compassionate heart for the needs of the sheep. The faithful shepherd searches diligently for any sheep who are scattered and labors to bring them back into the flock. Lord, grant each pastor the heart of a faithful shepherd.

What do you think? If a man has 100 sheep, and one of them goes astray, does he not leave the 99 and go to the mountains to seek the one that is straying? And if he should find it, assuredly, I say to you, he rejoices more over that sheep than over the 99 that did not go astray. Even so it is not the will of your Father who is in heaven that one of these little ones should perish (Matt 18:13–14).

CHAPTER 8

Seeking the Lost and Perishing

Matt Queen

As has been discussed already in this book, metaphors of *shepherds* and *sheep* abound in the Scriptures. These metaphors possess multiple referents. In the Old Testament, these metaphors depict (1) a ruler as *shepherd* and the nation of Israel or Judah as *sheep*, with some exceptions (e.g., Isa 44:28); (2) a prophet as *shepherd* and the congregation as *sheep*; or (3) Yahweh as *Shepherd* and Israel as His *sheep*.[1] As Walther Zimmerli explains of the *shepherd-sheep* metaphors in the Old Testament:

---

[1] Concerning the shepherd and sheep being representative of a ruler and his nation, Paul M. Joyce states, "Both the context here [Ezek 34:1] and usage elsewhere (e.g., 2 Sam 5:2; Isa 44:28) indicate that this ["shepherds"] is a reference to royal leaders. In the prophet's [Ezekiel's] explanation of the national disaster, judgement on the royal leaders of Judah plays a central part" (*Ezekiel: A Commentary*, Library of Hebrew Bible/Old Testament Studies 482 [New York: T&T Clark, 2007]196). John W. Wevers adds, "The designation of shepherd for ruler was widespread and a favorite throughout the Near East. . . . So too among the Hebrews. David, the ideal king of the Golden Age, was according to an old tradition a shepherd in his youth. Jeremiah in particular used the term to designate Judah's rulers" (*Ezekiel*, The New Century Bible Commentary [London: Nelson, 1969], 257). In his noteworthy work on the theological and sociopolitical implications of the shepherd motif in the Old Testament, Ignatius M. C. Obinwa concurs with both Joyce and Wevers by asserting, "[A]s in the Egyptian and Mesopotamian scripts . . . besides the real or ordinary meaning of tending livestock, the shepherd motif in the OT has two major metaphorical aspects, namely: *The metaphor of YHWH as shepherd with the Israelites as his flock and*

Both Israel's *kings* (David) and her *prophets* (Amos) . . . had direct contact with [the vocation of shepherd]. Thus the conventional language has been filled over and over with insight. In the OT too, in the first place, *Yahweh* can be addressed as the 'shepherd of Israel' . . . and his caring activity towards the people . . . and towards the individual . . . can be fully described in this image.[2]

The New Testament uses these metaphors with less variance. In the Gospels, *shepherd* denotes Jesus Christ, who is associated with the lost *sheep* of Israel, except in quoting Zech 13:7 when the reference to *sheep* refers to the disciples of Jesus (Matt 26:31; Mark 14:27). Outside the Gospels, *sheep* refers to believers in the church (Heb 13:20), whereas *shepherd* denotes either Christ (Heb 13:20; 1 Pet 1:25; 5:4; Rev 7:17) or a pastor (Acts 20:28; 1 Pet 5:2).

Does an aspect of these *shepherd-sheep* metaphors relate to a pastor-shepherd's responsibility to evangelize, as well as to lead his congregation to evangelize? If so, then how? This chapter endeavors to investigate to what extent, if any, the Old Testament imagery of seeking the lost and perishing, particularly in Ezek 34:4 and 16, can encourage and inform the evangelistic responsibilities of the contemporary pastor.

"Seeking the Lost and Perishing" in the Old Testament

Although the *lost/perishing* (Hb. *'avad*) *sheep* metaphor appears four times in the Old Testament (Ps 119:176; Jer 50:6; Ezek 34:4, 16), its association with the activity of *seeking* (Hb. *baqash*) occurs only in Ps 119:176 and Ezek 34:4, 16.[3] The word *'avad* can mean "lost, straying [or

---

the metaphor of the Israelite leaders as shepherds" ("*I Shall Feed Them with Good Pasture*" *(Ezek 34:14)—The Shepherd Motif in Ezekiel 34: Its Theological Import and Socio-Political Implications* (Würzburg, Germany: Echter, 2012), 233.

[2] Italics added for emphasis. Walther Zimmerli, *Ezekiel I*, trans. R. E. Clements, Hermeneia (Philadelphia: Fortress, 1979), 214.

[3] The word *'avad* (Hb., "lost, what was lost") describes all three *sheep* references in the qal. Concerning the use of *'avad* throughout the Old Testament, only in the qal do both meanings, "to perish" and "to wander off [or to be lost]," occur (Benedikt Otzen, "אָבַד," in *TDOT*, ed. G. Johannes Botterweck and Helmer Ringgren, trans. John T. Willis [Grand Rapids: Eerdmans, 1974; reprint, 1983], 1:20); Cornelius Van Dam, "אָבַד," in *NIDOTTE*, ed. Willem A. VanGemeren (Grand Rapids: Zondervan, 1997), 1:223–25.

wandering], or perishing." In these three cases, it figuratively describes erring men.[4] What, then, does *'avad* mean in these contexts, and how does its meaning describe the spiritual condition of its referents?

David confesses, "I have gone astray like a *lost* sheep; / *Seek* Your servant, / For I do not forget Your commandments" (Ps 119:176, italics added). While meditating on the Word, David acknowledges that his own sin has led him astray as a lost (*'avad*) sheep, and he implores Yahweh to seek (*baqash*) him.[5] Unlike the sheep that represent sinners who are perishing in their iniquities (Isa 53:6), David writes as someone who already embraces the Lord's precepts. In doing so, he realizes his predicament in temporarily wandering away from the law and asks the Lord to seek him that he might continue walking in the commandments. Throughout the psalm David identifies himself as a servant of the Lord who desires to walk in the way of Lord; therefore, "lost or wandering," rather than "perishing," most appropriately conveys the meaning of *'avad*, reflecting David's spiritual condition in this text.

Whereas David, because of his own sin of temporarily straying from following God's commandments, self-identifies as a "lost/wandering" sheep in Ps 119:176, the sheep metaphor differs somewhat in Ezek 34:4. "The weak [sheep] you [the shepherds of Israel] have not strengthened, nor have you healed those who were sick, nor bound up the broken, nor brought back what was driven away, nor *sought what was lost*; but with force and cruelty you have ruled them."[6] Ezekiel delivers his prophecy during the Babylonian exile. The sheep to whom he specifically refers in chapter 34 are the exiles of Judah and, perhaps, as John W. Wevers suggests, the dispersion of Israel in general.[7] Ezekiel 33:10 conveys the house of Israel's confession that their despairing condition has resulted from their own sin: "Therefore you, O son of man, say to the house of Israel: 'Thus you say, "If our transgressions and our sins lie upon us, and we pine away in them, how can we then live?"'"

---

[4] BDB, s.v. "אָבַד."
[5] Here, *'avad* functions as an attributive participle.
[6] Emphases and parenthetical phrases added for clarity.
[7] Wevers, *Ezekiel*, 259.

However, Ezekiel's next oracle, recorded in 34:4, shifts "to portray the people as more sinned against than sinning."[8] Because of the sheep's overall desperate condition recorded in both verses 4 and 16, "perishing" rather than "lost" seems to communicate the meaning of 'avad in these two occurrences.[9]

The "sheep" (Ezek 34:6) have been neglected by the "shepherds of Israel" (v. 2), the previous corrupt kings of Judah who have led the nation to its own ruin and exile.[10] As Lamar Cooper explains:

The indictment[s] against these shepherds [as recorded in Ezek 34:1–6 include:] First, they did not seek to meet the needs of the people but only used the people for their own selfish ends (vv. 2–3). Second they did not take special care of those in need, the helpless members of society. Rather they met weakness and injury with callous cruelty (v. 4). For lack of positive moral or spiritual leadership the people wandered from the Lord and became a prey to idolatry and immorality (vv. 5–6).[11]

Although they are the victims of the shepherds' sin, the sheep are not altogether innocent, as the previous oracle indicates in Ezek 33:10. C. F. Keil writes:

When we find this mournful fate of the people described as brought about by the bad shepherds, and attributable to faults of theirs, we must not regard the words as applying merely to the mistaken policy of the kings with regard to external affairs (Hitzig); for this was in itself simply a consequence of their neglect of their theocratic calling, and of their falling away from the Lord into idolatry. *It is*

---

[8] Moshe Greenberg, *Ezekiel 21–37: A New Translation with Introduction and Commentary*, Anchor Bible Series (New York: Doubleday, 1997), 698.

[9] In these verses, the word 'avad functions as a substantive participle.

[10] Conversely, Ronald M. Hals suggests that instead of referring to the previous evil kings of Judah, "Chapter 34 could by envisaged as a response to the despairing complaints within the exilic community about the folly of leaders like Zedekiah and Ishmael, the son of Nethaniah (Jeremiah 41), but that remains purely hypothetical." *Ezekiel*, ed. Rolf P. Knierim and Gene M. Tucker, The Forms of the Old Testament Literature (Grand Rapids: Eerdmans, 1989), 14:250.

[11] Lamar Eugene Cooper, *Ezekiel*, NAC, vol. 17 (Nashville: B&H, 1994), 300.

*true that the people had also made themselves guilty of this sin, so
that it was obliged to atone not only for the sins of its shepherds,
but for its own sin also*; but this is passed by here, in accordance
with the design of this prophecy.[12]

In what way could the sins of the shepherds and the sheep be atoned?

Ezekiel's prophecy turns from indicting the wicked shepherds to an-
ticipating a good and true Shepherd who will succeed in every way they
have failed (34:16). He declares: "*I will seek what was lost* and bring back
what was driven away, bind up the broken and strengthen what was sick;
but I will destroy the fat and the strong, and feed them in judgment" [em-
phasis added]. The good Shepherd's declaration of future action reverses
the order and structure of his charges against the wicked shepherds' past
actions (34:4). James A. Durlesser explains:

> [Verses 1–16 are] demarcated by an *inclusio*, the frames of which
> are in vv. 4 and 16. The contents of these two verses are arranged
> in an extended chiastic reversal. In v. 4, Ezekiel introduces a series
> of indictments, listing the ways in which the shepherds had failed
> in their duties. Verse 16 presents the same shepherding tasks—in
> reverse order—as examples of things that Yahweh is going to do
> on behalf of the flock.

v. 4   A. The ill you have not strengthened.

            The weak you have not healed.

       B. Those with broken bones—

            you have not bound them.

        C. The one gone astray

            you have not brought back.

         D. *The one lost you have not sought out.*

---

[12] Italics added. C. F. Keil, *Ezekiel, Daniel*, trans. James Martin, Keil & Delitzsch Commentary on the Old Testament, vol. 9 (Grand Rapids: Eerdmans reprint, 1978), 84.

v. 16   D'. *The one lost I am going to seek out.*

C'. And the one who has gone astray

I am going to lead back.

B'. Those with broken bones—

I am going to bind them.

A'. The weak I am going to make strong.[13]

The good Shepherd's work begins where the evil shepherds' failures end—*he will seek after the perishing and lost sheep.* In addition to correcting the failures of the evil shepherds, the good Shepherd will judge between those who are His sheep and those who are not His sheep: "Therefore I will save My flock, and they shall no longer be a prey; and *I will judge between sheep and sheep*" (Ezek 34:22, italics added). This particular judgment shares similarities with the forthcoming, eschatological judgment recorded in Matt 25:31–46.

Who is this good Shepherd coming both to shepherd His people and judge between them, fulfilling the prophetic anticipation of Ezekiel 34? Using language reminiscent of Ezekiel 34, Jesus declares, "I am the good Shepherd" (John 10:11). In addition, the *seeking lost/perishing sheep* language employed by Jesus in the Gospels of Matthew and Luke (Matt 18:10–14; Luke 15:1–7; cp. Luke 19:10) directly correlates with the language employed in Ezekiel 34, identifying Jesus as the good Shepherd. Consider the chapter's repetition of the word "seek" (Hb. *baqash*, "seek, search," vv. 4, 6, 16; and *darash*, "seek, search carefully, require," vv. 6, 8, 10–11), which Zimmerli regards as a "key-word," obviously indicative of the shepherd imagery employed of Jesus in the Gospels (e.g., Matt 18:12; cp. Luke 15:4).[14] In fact, Robert W. Jenson writes:

---

[13] Emphasis added. James A. Durlesser, *The Metaphorical Narratives in the Book of Ezekiel* (Lewiston, NY: The Edwin Mellon Press, 2006), 15–16. Moshe Greenburg concurs, "[Verses 11–16 portray] God's assumption of the shepherd's role and his reversal of the disastrous course of events, starting with the last and working backward." *Ezekiel 21–37*, The Anchor Bible (New York: Doubleday, 1997), 705.

[14] Zimmerli, *Ezekiel I*, 215.

Ezekiel 34:11–16 is a word of gospel that corresponds to the fore-going judgment. It reaches its climax with the eschatologically drastic promise: "I myself will be the shepherd of my sheep" (34:15). The Lord will personally do what Israel's rulers were sup-posed to do and did not and what Jesus in a parable (Matt 18:12 and parallels) describes as his own mission: the Lord will search for the lost sheep and bring them back.[15]

So, in what ways does Jesus Christ fulfill the Good Shepherd prophecy of Ezekiel 34 in both Matthew and Luke?

A Brief Consideration of the Use of "Seeking the Lost and Perishing" by Matthew and Luke

Shepherd-sheep language about Jesus in the Gospels (i.e., Matt 9:36; 15:24; 18:10–14; 25:31–46; Mark 6:34; 14:27; Luke 15:1–7; John 10:1–30) corresponds both with the good and true Shepherd of Ezekiel 34 and with the duties He will perform. Joachim Jeremias writes:

Not merely in Jn. 10, but in the Synoptic Gospel too, Jesus referred to Himself as the Messianic Shepherd promised in the OT . . . . He used the figure of speech in three ways:
a. To describe His mission He uses an ancient motif of world renewal, namely, that of gathering again the dispersed flock which is abandoned to destruction (Mt. 15:24; 10:6; . . . Lk. 19:10).
b. . . . [T]o intimate to the disciples His death and return (Mk. 14:27; Mt. 26:31; cf. Jn. 16:32).
c. . . . [To] illustrate the execution of eschatological judgement (Mt. 25:32).[16]

In exercising the first of these three uses, Jesus utilizes and/or alludes to the *seeking lost/perishing sheep* language of Ezekiel 34 in Matt 15:24

---

[15] Robert W. Jenson, *Ezekiel*, Brazos Theological Commentary of the Bible (Grand Rapids: Brazos, 2009), 265.

[16] Joachim Jeremias, "ποιμήν, […]," in *TDNT*, ed. Gerhard Kittel and Gerhard Friedrich, trans. Geoffrey W. Bromiley (Grand Rapids: Eerdmans, 1968), 6:492–93.

(cf. 10:5–15); 18:10–14; and Luke 15:1–7 (cf. 19:10). By doing so, he associates his mission with, as well as reveals his identity as, the good and true Shepherd of Ezekiel 34.

When a Syrophoenician woman implores Jesus to heal her demon-possessed daughter, Jesus answers her, "I was not *sent* except to the *lost sheep* of the house of Israel" (Matt 15:24) [emphasis added]. Upon first reading this statement, readers assume Jesus to be unwilling to minister to the woman because she is a Gentile and not a Jew. However, such a reading proves untenable, as Jesus does heal the woman's daughter in response to her faith in Jesus (Matt 15:28). Could his reply to the woman's voice be an assumption by some present there of Jesus's ministry focus to Jews alone, a view that he intends to correct? This perhaps is the case, but not likely. Craig L. Blomberg offers a more probable interpretation of the meaning of 15:24 in conjunction with Jesus's commission of the Twelve in Matt 10:6. He explains:

> Only Matthew includes . . . [the] distinctively particularist text ["But go rather to the lost sheep of the house of Israel"]. But these restrictions do not contradict the Great Commission (28:18–20). Even 10:18 anticipates the disciples going into Gentile territory. Instead, Jesus' commands fit the larger pattern of his own ministry prior to his death and match the missionary priority Paul himself maintained throughout Acts (e.g., 13:46; 18:6; 19:9; 28:25–28) and articulated in Rom 1:16 ("first for the Jew, and then for the Gentile").[17]

"Perhaps the same solution to the particularist-universalist tension [in 10:6] applies here [15:24]," he continues, adding later, "But more relevant to the immediate context, however, since Jesus has left Israel already [15:21], is the interpretation that takes these words as a test or prompt of some kind designed to draw out the woman into further discussion."[18] If this preferred interpretation is correct, then Jesus fulfills Ezekiel 34 as Shepherd to the sheep of Israel, while extending the good Shepherd's duties beyond Israel to include all who are lost and perishing.

---

[17] Craig L. Blomberg, *Matthew*, NAC (Nashville: B&H, 1992), 22:170.
[18] Ibid., 243.

The second reference of *seeking lost/perishing sheep* in the Gospels of Matthew and Luke occurs in both Matt 18:10–14 and Luke 15:1–7. In these texts Jesus employs the parable of the Lost Sheep while addressing groups despised in society or looked upon with suspicion. These groups include children (Matt 18:10), as well as tax collectors and sinners (Luke 15:1–2). In the parable, He describes a man who loses a sheep among his flock numbering 100. The man leaves the 99 sheep in search of the one that is lost. When he finds the lost sheep, he returns rejoicing over it. This parable explains the declaration of Jesus's mission and purpose, "For the Son of Man has come to save that which was lost" (Matt 18:11), a phrase repeated in Luke 19:10 in the context of salvation that comes to the house of Zacchaeus. In Luke 15:7, He likens the lost sheep to a sinner in need of repentance. By using the language of *seeking the lost/perishing sheep*, Jesus demonstrates the good Shepherd's "seeking what is perishing" as intentionally seeking those in need of God's salvation and calling them to receive it through repentance and faith.

The Rod and the Staff: Seeking the Lost

To what extent, therefore, does the Old Testament's use of "seeking the lost/perishing," particularly in Ezek 34:4 and 16, encourage and inform the evangelistic responsibilities of the contemporary pastor? In the introduction of this book, Deron J. Biles warns, "We must be careful not to press the image[ry of sheep and shepherd] too far. There are obvious limitations to the[se] images."[19] Ezekiel 34 uses *shepherd-sheep* language to deliver a word of condemnation against the sins of evil Jewish rulers (vv. 1–10), as well as a word of comfort for the Jewish people of exile (vv. 11–31). Given that the oracle in Ezekiel 34 was not originally addressed to today's pastors, can this passage of Scripture be used legitimately to encourage and inform contemporary pastors in their pastoral duties? Ezekiel 34 rightfully can be used without pressing the original intent of the text or the *shepherd-sheep* imagery beyond hermeneutical bounds for at least three reasons. First, embedded within the original intent of the oracle is a corpus of ministerial duties, which, by the

---

[19] See Introduction, "The Ministry of the Shepherd," 4.

symbolism of shepherding, applies to multiple referents, whether kings and rulers, prophets (though not in Ezekiel 34), or even Yahweh himself. Regarding verse 4, Paul M. Joyce says that "'you have not sought the lost' . . . is a beautiful expression of pastoral care (cp. v. 16), rather untypical of Ezekiel."[20] Second, in Matt 10:5–15 the good and true Shepherd, Jesus Christ, sends His disciples to the lost sheep of Israel as a connected extension of His fulfilling Ezek 34:16. In fact, His sending the disciples to the lost sheep includes a prioritized command, "And as you go, preach, saying, 'The kingdom of heaven is at hand'" (Matt 10:7). This occurrence, as well as other accounts in the Gospels (Matt 15:24; 18:10–14; Mark 6:34; Luke 19:10), equate "seeking the lost and perishing" with preaching the gospel of repentance to sinners. Last, the Shepherd provides pastors, in His absence until He returns (Heb 13:17, 20; 1 Pet 5:1–4), to lead the congregations in accordance with the *shepherd-sheep* model, which by implication includes "seeking the lost and perishing." Therefore, contemporary pastors who would perform their evangelistic duties should consider the reasons why they must seek the lost and perishing, be aware of impediments preventing them from seeking the lost and perishing, and adopt an intentional plan to assist them and their congregations to seek the lost and perishing.

Reasons Why Pastors Must Seek the Lost and Perishing

Pastors must seek the lost and perishing because the Bible commands it. Paul instructs the young pastor, Timothy, "[D]o the work of an evangelist" (2 Tim 4:5). Some pastors have mistakenly convinced themselves that only those with "the gift of evangelism" have the ability and the responsibility to evangelize; however, the Bible never describes "the gift of evangelism." Paul does identify "the gift of the evangelist" (Eph 4:11) but explains that these spiritually gifted evangelists equip the saints for ministry (Eph 4:12–13). As such, all believers are responsible to be equipped for ministry, which includes being equipped by those spiritually gifted evangelists to evangelize.

Also, *pastors must seek the lost and perishing because their congregations will not follow where they do not lead.* Frequently, pastors

---

[20] Joyce, *Ezekiel: A Commentary*, 196.

underestimate the influence they hold in their congregations. Congregations reflect their pastors. Generally, congregations value the things that their pastors hold important. If the members of churches never see or hear of their pastors' evangelizing, their pastors will rarely, if ever, see or hear of their congregants' evangelizing.

Impediments to Pastors Who Would Seek the Lost and Perishing

Most, if not all, Bible-believing pastors believe they should seek the lost and perishing; however, not all of them do so. Although many reasons could be offered to explain their negligence, perhaps a number of them convince themselves they are evangelistic when they are not. How can pastors avoid convincing themselves they are more evangelistic than they are?

First, *pastors must not allow their past evangelistic activities to compensate for present periods of evangelistic inactivity.* Most pastors' routines will fluctuate in the frequency of their many pastoral duties, including their shepherding duty to evangelize. This phenomenon results from the daily, multiple tasks required of shepherd-pastors (i.e., feeding the sheep, caring for the sick, and going after the scattered), constraining their schedules and making it genuinely difficult to fulfill all of their duties. Evangelism is often relegated to the end of ministerial to-do lists. This reality lures pastors to convince themselves that past evangelistic activity will compensate for their current evangelistic inactivity. Pastors will find that failing to plan time to evangelize will result in failing to find time to evangelize. Pastors who would seek the lost and perishing must strive to schedule evangelism concurrently with the execution of their daily shepherding activities.

Second, *pastors must not limit their evangelism to their sermons.* Sermons serve as one, if not the most obvious, way for pastors to evangelize. The lost and perishing attend virtually every venue where pastors feed their flocks by preaching the Word. Because a pastor cannot know the spiritual condition of everyone under the sound of his voice, he must ensure that he seeks the lost and perishing in each of the sermons he preaches. Pastors should also remind themselves that in the New Testament, Jesus, Peter, Philip, and Paul all evangelized both by their public preaching and through their personal conversations. Inasmuch as shepherd-pastors sincerely desire to follow these New Testament paragons while seeking the

lost from their pulpits, they will also convince themselves of the dual necessity in seeking the lost in their steps on the pavements of life.

Third, *pastors whose churches employ staff members to lead in evangelism must not relinquish their own evangelistic responsibilities to those
staff members*. As mentioned earlier, belief that the Holy Spirit bestows a
"gift of evangelism" exclusively upon a select group of believers to carry
out the work of evangelism gains increasing acceptance today. However,
the Bible does not mention a "gift of evangelism." Rather than suggest a
spiritual "gift of evangelism" for a select few, Scripture presents evangelism as a spiritual discipline required of all believers. Nevertheless, Paul
does identify the "gift of evangelists" (Eph 4:11), who would equip all
saints for ministry along with the apostles, prophets, pastors, and teachers
(Eph 4:12–13). In the contemporary context, Christ continues to equip
believers for ministry through evangelists, pastors, and teachers.[21]

Churches that desire the total participation of their membership in
evangelism will employ a vocational or voluntary staff evangelist for the
purpose of equipping and encouraging evangelism. In churches that do
so, pastors must overcome any temptation to abdicate their evangelistic
leadership among the congregation to the evangelist. No matter how much
charisma, giftedness, and respect staff evangelists may possess, congregations ultimately follow the headship and example of their lead pastors.
Thus, even as all believers are responsible for reaching the lost, the pastor
must model that obedience for those with whom he serves. Moreover, as
noted above, Paul charged Timothy directly, and subsequent pastors by
extension, with the responsibility to "do the work of an evangelist" (2 Tim
4:5), making it a command. The most effective and consistent churches
who seek the lost and perishing utilize ministry teams that include pastors
who champion evangelism and staff evangelists who equip and encourage
evangelism under the direction of their shepherd.

Last, *pastors must not confuse evangelism with marketing*. Numerous
churches use advertising and/or branding in order to increase attendance

---

[21] For an exegetical, theological, and historical explanation on the omission of apostles
and prophets in the contemporary context, consult John A. Crabtree, "A Critique of David
Cannistraci's Understanding of the Gift of the Apostle and the Emerging Apostolic Movement," *The Journal of the American Society for Church Growth* 10 (Fall 1999): 47–57.

at their services and events. Marketing can greatly assist churches in the work of their ministry in many ways. However, pastors may face the temptation to believe that marketing campaigns are the same as, if not a viable substitute for, evangelism. They would do well to remind themselves of some differences between the two strategies. Marketing seeks people to impress: evangelism seeks souls to implore. Marketing pitches sales; evangelism invites sinners. Marketing appeals to the eye; evangelism makes appeals with the mouth. Marketing concerns itself with what others want to hear; evangelism conveys what God, in His Word, has spoken. Pastors should not feel guilty if they use marketing strategies for their churches, as long as they do not replace evangelism with marketing and continue to seek the lost through evangelism.

Suggestions for Pastors Who Desire to Seek the Lost and Perishing

Pastors who would seek the lost and perishing should consider the following ways to meet their own responsibilities to evangelize, as well as lead their congregations to evangelize.

First, *pastors should practice intentional evangelism.* Evangelism does not occur by accident. It may not always take place according to a pastor's plans, but evangelism does happen when he plans it. Pastors who find difficulty making evangelism an intentional part of their daily routine should consider self-examining the value they place on lost and perishing souls. While explaining from Ezekiel 34 why shepherd-pastors must seek after those who are lost and perishing, Biles recalls one writer's illustration of an "un-lost credit card."[22] Upon losing his credit card, this man directs all his attention and effort toward locating it. Feeling no preoccupation with the other "un-lost" cards in his wallet, he goes on a search for his lost card with a desperately urgent obsession. In similar fashion, pastors will find a correlation between the value they place on lost and perishing

---

[22] Deron J. Biles, "The Good of the One vs. The Good of the Many," *Theological Matters* blog of Southwestern Baptist Theological Seminary, July 14, 2016, http://theologicalmatters.com/2013/06/13/2517/. In this article, Biles refers to an illustration made by Andy Stanley in *Deep and Wide: Creating Churches Unchurched People Love to Attend* (Grand Rapids: Zondervan, 2012), 294–95.

souls and the urgency they have in seeking the lost and perishing through evangelism. Second, *pastors should articulate the evangelistic expectations they have of their congregations.* Charles Roesel, retired pastor of First Baptist Church in Leesburg, Florida, says, "People do not tend to drift toward evangelism, but drift away from it. Leaders must continually call the members back to evangelism."[23] Pastors must avoid assuming their congregants (1) know their pastor's evangelistic expectations and (2) will evangelize without being reminded of their pastor's evangelistic expectations. Not all church members know, thus they will not meet, their pastor's evangelistic expectations. When pastors generally communicate their expectations, whether evangelistic or not, their staff and lay leadership usually do not hear them until the pastor gets tired of repeating them. Furthermore, only when staff and lay leadership repeat expectations so many times that they grow tired of reiterating them do the majority of the laity actually begin to hear and understand those expectations. Pastors whose churches understand and meet their evangelistic expectations are those who frequently reiterate them and encourage the same of their staff and lay leadership.

Third, *pastors should find ways to identify and encourage members of their churches who evangelize.* Church members respond to their pastors' encouragement. Ask church members to keep you informed about their personal soul-winning activities. When they do, consider sharing a brief testimony from the pulpit of how members actively share the gospel. Pray for the lost people they are seeking through evangelism. Send a brief note or e-mail periodically to show them your appreciation for their faithful evangelism.

Fourth, *pastors should lead their congregations to intercede publicly for the lost.* Studies conducted in the last 20 years consistently have found that churches considered most effective in their evangelism publicly pray for the salvation of unbelievers by name.[24] Of course, when leading their congregations in public prayer for the lost, pastors must exercise wisdom

---

[23] Steve R. Parr, Steve Foster, and Tom Crites, *Georgia's Top Evangelistic Churches: Ten Lessons from the Most Effective Churches* (Duluth: Georgia Baptist Convention, 2008), 7.

[24] Consult Thom Rainer, *Effective Evangelistic Churches: Successful Churches Reveal What Works and What Doesn't* (Nashville: B&H, 1996) and Parr, Foster, and Crites, *Georgia's Top Evangelistic Churches.*

and sensitivity so as not to embarrass the unbelievers. Consider explaining that churches pray for all people, regardless of their spiritual condition, and that to do otherwise would not be compassionate and caring. In addition, enlist members who became believers as a result of the consistent public prayers and personal witness of church members to lead in these public prayer times as a testimony to this practice.

Last, *pastors should invite the lost to receive Christ publicly.* Pastors can, and should, publicly invite unbelievers to repent, believe, and confess Jesus Christ as Lord without manipulating or pressuring them into making false decisions. Effective text-driven preachers who seek the lost and perishing do not tack on invitations to the end of their sermons, rather their calls for sinners to repent and believe Christ naturally flow from the textual application. Public evangelistic invitations can take many forms, from pastors instructing unbelievers to come to them during services or after services, to completing and submitting information on a card for a subsequent meeting, to exiting the sanctuary quietly to spiritual counseling rooms.

Conclusion

In 1869, famed hymn-writer Fannie Crosby visited a New York mission. During her visit, she informally addressed a group of workers. As she spoke, she felt an overwhelming sense that one of the men in attendance must be rescued from sin and death. She pled with the men, not knowing, that one of them had wandered from his mother's teaching and needed to receive Christ as his Savior and Lord that very day. After she spoke, an 18-year-old young man came to her and asked, "Ma'am, were you talking to me?" She replied, "Have you left your mother's teaching? Do you need Christ?" He indicated that he did and, standing there with her, received Christ as his Savior and Lord. Not long after this encounter, Crosby penned "Rescue the Perishing":

> Rescue the perishing, care for the dying,
> Snatch them in pity from sin and the grave;
> Weep o'er the erring one, lift up the fallen,
> Tell them of Jesus, the mighty to save.

***

Rescue the perishing, duty demands it;
Strength for thy labor the Lord will provide;
Back to the narrow way patiently win them;
Tell the poor wand'rer a Savior has died.

***

Though they are slighting Him, still He is waiting,
Waiting the penitent child to receive;
Plead with them earnestly, plead with them gently;
He will forgive if they only believe.

***

Down in the human heart, crushed by the tempter,
Feelings lie buried that grace can restore;
Touched by a loving heart, wakened by kindness,
Chords that were broken will vibrate once more.
Rescue the perishing, care for the dying,
Jesus is merciful, Jesus will save!

Roy Fish tells that some years after Crosby penned this hymn, L. R. Scarborough was preaching a revival meeting. Each afternoon during the revival, he and the pastor had been soul-winning. One day, they encountered two young men with whom they shared the gospel and had invited to receive Christ. Although the boys were unwilling to receive Christ then, they promised to come to the meeting that night. They arrived that night and sat near the front of the church. Scarborough preached in the power of the Spirit and called the lost to receive Christ. As the public invitation was extended, the congregation sang Crosby's "Rescue the Perishing." Upon singing the words, "Snatch them in pity, from sin and the grave," Scarborough was overcome with a burden for these two boys who would perish without Christ. He exited the platform with tears in his eyes and walked down to where the boys were standing, visibly under the Spirit's conviction. After he led them to Christ, someone in the back of the church shouted, "Lee, don't get too excited, it's just a song!" Scarborough was not excited over a song—he was overjoyed, as are all shepherds seeking the lost and perishing, when the good and true Shepherd finds His lost sheep and rescues them from perishing.

CHAPTER 9

Leading the Flock

Fred Luter

I will never forget the day I was called to be the pastor of Franklin Avenue Baptist Church in New Orleans, Louisiana. After sending in my résumé several months before, and after meeting with the pulpit committee three times, I was finally given an invitation to meet the members of this mission church of about 45 members.

My assignment was to teach a joint Sunday School class and then preach at the 11:00 a.m. worship service. After the worship service, there was a cake-and-punch reception planned in the church fellowship hall so that I could meet the congregation and they could meet my wife, Elizabeth, and our two children, who were four and two years old at the time.

After the time of meet-and-greet in the fellowship hall, we all met back in the sanctuary for a Q & A time from the church members. For an hour and a half I answered every question, to the best of my ability and experience, about what I would do if I were to be called as the pastor of the church. At the end of the interview time with the congregation, the pulpit committee thanked me and said that they would contact me later on that evening with the results of the vote.

About two hours after leaving the interview, I received the phone call. By a unanimous vote, the church had called me to become the pastor of Franklin Avenue Baptist Mission! It was a moment I will never forget.

After coming off that truly exciting moment in my life, reality started setting in. I had never before been a pastor of a church. After my salvation and call to the ministry, I was a street preacher sharing the gospel of Jesus Christ every Saturday on different street corners of the neighborhood in which I grew up—the Lower Ninth Ward in New Orleans. Besides that, as an associate minister of a local church, I had preached from a church pulpit only two or three times a year. Now that I had been called to be the pastor of a church, I would be expected not only to preach every Sunday but also to teach a Bible study on Wednesday night, as well as perform a number of other duties listed on my job description.

For a young first-time shepherd, this role can be a very intimidating assignment. However, I am convinced that God will never call you to do something without equipping you to do it. Therefore, for the rest of this chapter I want to share seven things that I was convicted to do when I began "leading the flock" at Franklin Avenue Baptist Church.

Be Faithful to God

Jeremiah 3:15

If you are going to lead the flock, you must be faithful to God. He is the one who called you to be a shepherd and entrusted to you the care of His people. God promised to give His people shepherds according to His heart, shepherds who would feed them with knowledge and understanding (Jer 3:15).

As a pastor, you must realize that your commitment, dedication, and hope is in God and God alone—not to the trustees, not to the deacons, not to relatives, or to families who are big givers in the church. Your number one priority as a shepherd is to give reverence and obedience to the one who called you—almighty God.

Now some of you may say that faithfulness to God should be a given in every shepherd's life. Yes, that should be true; however, I have seen so many preachers and pastors compromise their faithfulness to God for various reasons. All of us know preachers and pastors who started out well but somewhere along the line were distracted by various attacks of the enemy. Brothers who were talented, gifted, and had tremendous potential have fallen to the tempting tactics of our common enemy. Some of them have lost their effectiveness as preachers, their position in the church, and, in a number of cases, their own families. That is why we must never take for granted how important it is to maintain an intimate, personal, and fulfilling relationship with God.

Another way that pastors can be faithful to God is to have a healthy fear of God, to the point that they think twice about the decisions they make. We, as shepherds, must have a conviction that we have to answer to God for everything we do.

Many can remember reaching high school years and going to activities with friends and classmates on your own. Before you would leave the house, perhaps one of your parents would charge you to "remember your last name." What they meant was that you needed to remember who you represented as you went out with your classmates. I believe every shepherd should have that same mind-set as he ministers in this sin-sick society. Everywhere you go you should always remember *whom* you represent. You represent Jehovah God Almighty! Therefore, you should be faithful to Him in every area of your life. I like Paul's words in his letter to the Romans: "Who shall separate us from the love of Christ?" (Rom 8:35). I am convinced that God will keep us, if we want to be kept. One of the most important decisions a shepherd can make to lead his flock is to be faithful to God.

Be Faithful to God's Word

2 Timothy 4:2

If you are going to lead the flock, you must be faithful to God's Word. Every shepherd is called to preach the Word of God. He is not called to expound upon the latest in politics or sports or even current events. When a pastor stands behind the pulpit, the people have a right to expect to hear the Word of God. Paul told Timothy:

Preach the word! Be ready in season and out of season. Convince, rebuke, exhort, with all longsuffering and teaching. For the time will come when they will not endure sound doctrine, but according to their own desires, because they have itching ears, they will heap up for themselves teachers; and they will turn their ears away from the truth, and be turned aside to fables. (2 Tim 4:2–4)

You do not have to be a rocket scientist to realize that we are living in the day and time Paul described. Mankind seems to be pulling further and further away from God and the ways of God. Listen to Paul's prophecy about the days in which we are living (2 Tim 3:1–5):

But know this, that in the last days perilous times will come: For men will be lovers of themselves, lovers of money, boasters, proud, blasphemers, disobedient to parents, unthankful, unholy, unloving, unforgiving, slanderers, without self-control, brutal, despisers of good, traitors, headstrong, haughty, lovers of pleasure rather than lovers of God, having a form of godliness but denying its power.

Wow, what an accurate picture of today's society! What an accurate picture of our cities. What an accurate picture of our communities. What an accurate picture of our culture. So here is the question: What is it going to take to change today's society—to change lives, to change morals, to change values, and to change mind-sets?

Well, let me ask: What did it take to change you? Before you were saved, before you were a seminary student, before you were a preacher, before you were a pastor, before you were who you are today . . . What did it take to change you?

The answer is that at some point in your life you heard the gospel. You heard the Word of God. Maybe it was at a church service, maybe in a Sunday school class, maybe at a revival service, or maybe at an evangelism conference. Once you heard the Word of God, your life was transformed. The Word of God changed your life! Paul testified about the gospel when he said, "For I am not ashamed of the gospel of Christ, for it is the power of God to salvation for everyone who believes" (Rom 1:16).

That is why I am convinced that if pastors are going to be effective in leading the flock, they must be faithful to God's Word. They must do all they can—spiritually, mentally, and physically—to prepare themselves to preach the Word of God. Again, Paul's advice to Timothy proves this point: "Be diligent to present yourself approved to God, a worker who does not need to be ashamed, rightly dividing the word of truth" (2 Tim 2:15). Make sure that you do all you can to pray, plan, prepare, and preach the Word of God as you lead the flock that He has assigned to you. One of the most important decisions a shepherd can make to lead his flock is to be faithful to God's Word.

Be Faithful to Your Family

1 Timothy 3:4; Ephesians 5:25

If a shepherd is going to be effective in leading the flock of God, he first must be effective in leading his own family. You must be faithful to your family. One of the problems I have seen in pulpits all over America is that too many pastors are putting the church before their families. I tell young pastors all the time that God will take care of His church. As a matter of fact, if you think that the church cannot go on without you—die. I assure you someone will be preaching in the pulpit next Sunday. But you cannot be replaced in your family.

The Bible is clear that as men of God we must make our families a priority. In Paul's letters to the church in Ephesus and to Timothy he admonished the church leaders to love their wives as Christ loves the church (Eph 5:25) and to have their children in submission (1 Tim 3:4). There is no way you can pull off either of those responsibilities if you do not take time with your family. Every shepherd needs to be convinced that his family is his first ministry.

Because your family is your first ministry, you need to share that information with the leadership and congregation where you serve as shepherd. They need to understand that if your son has a soccer game on the same night as a deacons meeting, you will be attending your son's soccer game. They need to understand that if your daughter has a recital on the night of a committee meeting, you will be attending your daughter's recital. They need to understand that if your wedding anniversary is the same night as a scheduled business meeting, that the meeting should be rescheduled or you will not be able to attend. I assure you, when pastors make that kind of commitment to their families, it will be a win-win for both the pastor's family and the church. Sometimes the shepherd is so busy trying to minister to the flock that his own family is neglected. Maybe that's why we sometimes hear that the pastor's kids are the worst kids in the church. Shepherds, make sure that is never the case for your family. They are your flock, too.

I try to model this when I preach. I begin each message by giving honor to the Lord and then to my wife, who often travels with me. Anyone who has heard me preach will recognize how I refer to my wife as "the love of my life, the apple of my eye, my prime rib, my good thing."

This kind of commitment to your family must be explained when you are first being considered as pastor of a church. You should communicate your commitment to your family with the pulpit committee during the interview process and then with the leadership when you are called. Not only will your decision honor your obedience to the Word of God, but it will also be a tremendous testimony and example to the members of the congregation. Moreover, long before you share your commitment with the pulpit committee, your family should know how committed you are to each of them.

As a young pastor, I made that decision early on in my ministry. I shared with my family that I would not take any preaching engagements other than my church on any of their birthdays or on my wedding anniversary. Because I was a product of parents who were divorced and suffered the consequences of it, I wanted to break that cycle in my own family. I did not have a dad in my home growing up, and I made a lot of bad decisions that I regret today. For kids to be what they have never seen is so hard. Therefore, I wanted my son to grow up in a home where he saw his dad loving his mom as Christ loved the church. In like manner, I wanted my daughter to grow up in a home where she saw what a godly man looks like when it comes to how he treats his wife. Both my son and daughter are now adult Christians living for God, and both are very involved in their local churches. As a matter of fact, my son is now a pastor of a church himself. I have no doubt that for each of them, their commitment to God is a direct result of the commitment that I made to them when they were kids growing up in our home.

In a day and time when the divorce rates among Christian couples are not much better than among couples without Christ, there is a great need for the shepherd to demonstrate how to be faithful to his family. The enemy knows that strong families make strong churches. So, in addition to the pastor's demonstrating his commitment to his family, the church should offer classes that can help every family to grow spiritually. It is the responsibility of the church to equip every member of a family to be able to carry out the respective roles that God designed for each of them. What a blessing that would be to see pastors setting the example for the church in this critical area. One of the most important decisions a shepherd can make to lead his flock is to be faithful to his family.

Be Faithful to the Church You Are Leading

1 Corinthians 15:58

To be called as a shepherd of a local congregation is one of the greatest honors in a minister's life. After reading your resume, going through the interview process, and hearing you preach the Word of God, a congregation comes together and calls you as the spiritual leader and visionary of that church—what a great honor that is! I am convinced that when a preacher is called as shepherd of a congregation, he needs to have a made-up mind that he will be at that church for the rest of his ministry. In other words, a preacher should not allow a church to call him as shepherd if he still has a resume in his back pocket looking for a bigger church.

Paul's advice is applicable here: "Therefore, my beloved brethren, be steadfast, immovable, always abounding in the work of the Lord, knowing that your labor is not in vain in the Lord" (1 Cor 15:58). A shepherd needs to be faithful to the church that he is leading.

When I was called as pastor of Franklin Avenue Baptist Church, I was committed to be at that church for the rest of my life. Even though we were a mission church with only 45 members, I was committed to do all I could do to help grow that church. Even though our physical church was located in "the hood," I just believed that if we as a congregation would be obedient to the Word of God, our church could grow. And God blessed that commitment!

I made it known that as the spiritual leader of that flock, I was there for the long haul. When I began accepting preaching engagements at larger churches across the country, some of our older members had concerns about another church "stealing" me away from Franklin Avenue. However, I was always up-front with them about my commitment to the congregation where I was serving. I wanted to make known that I was faithful to the church that I was leading.

My faithfulness to the church was truly tested after Hurricane Katrina flooded the city of New Orleans in August 2005. When all the citizens of our city were forced to evacuate, we were scattered all across America. My wife, Elizabeth, and I settled in Birmingham, Alabama, where our daughter was a student at Samford University. When we had evacuated the city in the past, we were normally only gone for about two days. However, when the levees broke and our city was flooded, those two days turned into seven months.

After the storm passed we found out that 80 percent of our city was under water. We soon learned that our home was flooded with five feet of water and our church sanctuary was submerged under nine feet of water. Because of the massive damage to properties all over the city of New Orleans, many of us were left with a decision we had never had to face before: Should we return to New Orleans? Many folk from New Orleans decided not to return and are now resettled in cities all over America. Among that number of people who relocated to other cities were a number of former shepherds in our city.

Because I was born and reared in New Orleans, I never thought about not returning to the city that I loved. In like manner, I never thought about not returning to rebuild Franklin Avenue Baptist Church. Even though I was offered the opportunity to shepherd other churches in Birmingham and Atlanta, I was convinced that my ministry was not done in New Orleans. I knew I had to go back and help to rebuild our church and our city.

As a result of having so many of our church members relocated to Houston, Texas, and Baton Rouge, Louisiana, we started churches in both of those cities. I appointed two of our associate ministers to shepherd those flocks, who were already meeting every weekend. We also had a group of members meeting at First Baptist Church of New Orleans, one of the few churches that did not flood in our city. Therefore, as a result of Katrina, we now had three different congregations worshiping in three different cities. I tell folk that before Hurricane Katrina we were the "church gathered"; after Hurricane Katrina we were the "church scattered."

While living in Birmingham, Elizabeth and I would drive the five hours every first and third Saturday to preach at the worship services in New Orleans and Baton Rouge on Sunday morning before driving back to Birmingham that afternoon. On every second and fourth Saturday we would drive the 11 hours one way to Houston to preach at the worship services in Houston on Sunday morning before driving back to Birmingham. We kept this schedule up for seven months until we started having worship services every Sunday morning in New Orleans. When people ask me why I kept such a hectic schedule for all of those months, the answer was easy. I love the members of the congregation of Franklin Avenue Baptist Church. They took a chance on me when they called me as their shepherd even though I had no pastoral experience. I pray that my actions proved my love and appreciation for this congregation. Most of all, I pray that I glorified the Lord by my faithfulness to the church I was leading. One of the most important decisions a shepherd can make to lead his flock is to be faithful to the church you are leading.

Be Faithful Through Your Lifestyle

Ephesians 4:1

Every shepherd has a bull's-eye on his chest. The enemy will do everything he can to get pastors and preachers to fall. Satan knows if he can get a shepherd to fall, the effects will be felt throughout the church locally and even universally. Therefore it should be a priority in every preacher's ministry to be faithful through his lifestyle. I love the challenge that Paul gives us in Eph 4:1, "I, therefore, the prisoner of the Lord, beseech you to walk worthy of the calling with which you were called." This challenge is critical in the life of every preacher because our calling is from God. We need to understand that we represent God in everything that we do. In other words, our lifestyles matter to God.

This fact is proved as we read about the qualifications of a shepherd in 1 Tim 3:1–7. What I find amazing about this text is that it says nothing about the minister's preaching style. It does not say if his style should be expository or topical. It does not say if he should be dressed in a suit and tie or in a golf shirt and slacks. It does not say if he should stand behind a pulpit or sit on a raised stool. The fact of the matter is that our lifestyles will speak a lot louder than our particular pulpit styles. The old saying is true: people would rather see a sermon than hear one.

Whenever a young man wants to speak with me about a "calling" on his life into the ministry, the first thing I ask him is how does his lifestyle line up with the qualifications of a shepherd in 1 Tim 3:1–7? Is he

blameless, the husband of one wife, temperate, sober-minded, of good behavior, hospitable, able to teach; not given to wine, not violent, not greedy for money, gentle, not quarrelsome, not covetous; one who rules his own house well, having his children in submission with all reverence (for if a man does not know how to rule his own house, how will he take care of the church of God?); not a novice, lest being puffed up with pride he fall into the same condemnation as the devil[?]

Moreover does he "have a good testimony among those who are outside, lest he fall into reproach and the snare of the devil"? These are the kinds of questions every minister must face.

Preachers should always be on guard because we never know when the enemy will attack. That is why every shepherd needs to have some personal convictions and principles that will not allow him to be put in a position where he can easily be tempted by the enemy. Decisions like personal counseling sessions alone with a female or involving himself directly with church finances should be avoided in the life of every preacher. No matter how long you have been saved or how long you have been in the ministry, you must do all that you can to avoid temptation as well as the appearance of evil. God through the power of the Holy Spirit can keep you; however, you must want to be kept. Never allow your effectiveness in the pulpit to be compromised by your lifestyle outside of the pulpit. One of the most important decisions a shepherd can make to lead his flock is to be faithful through his lifestyle.

Be Faithful During the Good Days

Psalm 122:1

During the 29 years I have been the pastor of Franklin Avenue Baptist Church in New Orleans, Louisiana, by God's grace we have had a lot of good days! The good days started at our church as a result of tremendous church growth—from a congregation that started out as a mission church with 45 members, to a membership that, before Hurricane Katrina flooded our city, was nearing 8,000. Yes, we have had a lot of good days. That is why each and every Sunday I felt like David when he said, "I was glad when they said to me, / 'Let us go into the house of the LORD'" (Ps 122:1). We started out small, but I assured those initial 45 members that I had no doubt our church could grow if we made a commitment in three areas.

I challenged our church, first of all, to be committed to biblical authority. If we were going to grow, then we had to be people who were committed to the Word of God. I have seen too many churches never reach their God-given potential because they have never trusted in and depended on God's Word. Many were more committed to man-made traditions than to the Bible.

One example of this was when I was first called as pastor of Franklin Avenue Mission. I discovered that the membership supplemented paying their bills by selling chicken dinners every Friday and Saturday. The congregation felt that because they only had a handful of faithful members, this was the only way to meet their monthly financial obligations. Knowing I should not start making changes right away, I started teaching a series on Christian stewardship at our Wednesday night Bible study, which included an emphasis on supporting the church through tithes and offerings. At the end of my second year as pastor I challenged our membership, which had grown to about 150 members, to trust God and His Word with our giving. I challenged the church to stop selling chicken dinners and begin demonstrating our faith in the Lord and obedience to Him through our tithes and offerings. I also challenged our ministry leaders to lead the way in their giving. I then made them a promise. My promise was that if in the first three months of the year we did not raise the funds needed for our monthly obligations through tithes and offerings, then I would be the first member to put on an apron and start frying chickens for the dinners. I never had to wear an apron because God did what His Word promised and provided our financial needs.

The second area to which I challenged our church to be committed was the discipleship of men. I told the congregation that if we were going to grow, we had to intentionally disciple and develop men. Our congregation was made up of 98 percent women and children. Since I had seen the difference it made to lead my family spiritually, I wanted to see the same thing happen at the church I was leading. I had the conviction that if you reach the man, you reach his entire family. I love the way Joshua said it: "But as for me, and my house, we will serve the LORD" (Josh 24:15). Therefore, we made reaching men a priority at Franklin Avenue. We used every idea we knew to reach men—especially athletic events, including basketball tournaments, Super Bowl fellowships, and hosting pay-per-view boxing matches at private homes. At some point during each event, we presented the gospel and gave men an opportunity to respond. We would then invite those men to our Sunday worship service.

The response was so great that men began inviting other men to our church. Every week during my announcements I would make a big deal about all the men in the church that Sunday. As a result of our faithfulness in the area of intentionally reaching men, our worship services now consistently average around 47 percent men in attendance! And because of that I say, "To God be the glory!"

The third area in which I challenged our congregation was in their commitment to evangelism. I told the congregation that if we were going to grow, everyone had to get involved in sharing the gospel. I discovered an evangelism strategy called *FRANgelism*, which is an acronym for: Friends, Relatives, Associates, and Neighbors.

The way *FRANgelism* works is first recognizing that everyone in the church has a lost or unchurched Friend, a lost or unchurched Relative, a lost or unchurched Associate/coworker, and a lost or unchurched Neighbor. After teaching members a series of Bible study classes on how to share their testimonies, I would challenge everyone to share his testimony with that lost friend, relative, associate, and neighbor, and then invite him to our church. On Sunday, our congregation would roll out the red carpet and treat our first-time guests like they were royalty. As a result of our praying, praise, music, worship, and preaching, the Lord added weekly to the church.

FRANgelism is how our church grew from 200 to almost 8,000. Again I say, "To God be the glory!" It was exciting to come to church each and every Sunday. Yes, those were certainly good days! One of the most important decisions a shepherd can make to lead his flock is to be faithful during the good days.

Be Faithful During the Difficult Days

2 Corinthians 4:8–10

As a disciple of Jesus Christ, you will find out that this journey of life is not exempt from the difficult and trying times. As a child of God, you will soon discover that trouble, trials, and tribulation are a part of the enemy's plan to get us discouraged so that we turn our backs on God. As you search the Scriptures, you will see that every follower of God had to deal with some sort of attack while representing God. However, in the midst of it all, God expects His sons and daughters to be faithful. Paul describes it like this: "We are hard-pressed on every side, yet not crushed; we are perplexed, but not in despair; persecuted, but not forsaken; struck down, but not destroyed—always carrying about in the body the dying of the Lord Jesus, that the life of Jesus also may be manifested in our body" (2 Cor 4:8–10).

Yes, difficult days will come in the life of every pastor, but you need to have the conviction that you will be faithful through it all. Even Jesus warned us about these times in the life of every believer when He told us, "These things I have spoken to you, that in Me you may have peace. In the world you will have tribulation; but be of good cheer, I have overcome the world" (John 16:33).

As a pastor, I have often said I am not surprised when the enemy attacks; however, what does surprise me is who the enemy uses. Through the difficult times of my ministry as a shepherd, I have always been amazed that members who gave me the toughest times were the ones I never expected to do so. Whether it was because of a decision I made, a sermon I preached, or a statement I made at a business meeting, I was always surprised from whom the opposition would arise.

On one occasion I had had enough. I had made up in my mind that I was going to confront a certain member at our next business meeting and give him a piece of my mind. The night before the meeting, God spoke to me as clear as the morning day that "this, too, shall pass." He reminded me that Jesus personally handpicked 12 disciples; yet out of that group, one betrayed him, one denied him, and one doubted that he had risen from the dead. God was telling me that if difficult days could happen to Jesus, I was not exempt. The next day I chose the Matthew 18 principle of dealing with difficult people. I called the brother and invited him to lunch. We talked, shared our hearts, apologized to each other for what we had heard about what someone thought we said about each other, prayed together, and worked out our differences. I even paid for lunch. As we left, we both testified that nobody was mad but the devil.

Let me share one final note about being faithful during difficult times. Shepherds should never—I repeat, never—use the pulpit and the preaching moment to get back at someone who has hurt you. Use that preaching time to rightly divide the Word of truth so God will be glorified, the saints of God will be edified, and lost sinners will come to repentance. I love the way David encouraged believers facing difficult times when he said, "Many are the afflictions of the righteous; / But the Lord delivers him out of them all" (Ps 34:19). Amen! Amen! Amen! One of the most important decisions a shepherd can make to lead his flock is to be faithful during the difficult days.

The Rod and the Staff: Being a Faithful Shepherd

I was blessed by the Lord and entrusted by the Southern Baptist Convention (SBC) to serve as their first African-American convention president. During those two years, I visited with as many churches, associations, state conventions, seminaries, colleges, and entities as my schedule would permit. Many of those were places an SBC President had never been before. In addition to my other responsibilities in that role, there were numerous emails, requests for book endorsements, media requests for interviews, as well as international travel. Plus, I sought never to neglect my most important roles as a husband, father, and pastor.

In reflecting on my two terms as SBC President, I think I was able to foster more diversity in our denomination with meetings throughout our convention and across the country. I see more ethnic participation in our denomination than ever before. Recently, the North American Mission Board (NAMB) has reported that from 1998 to 2011, African-American church plants increased by 82.7 percent.

Today, I continue to serve our denomination as the National African-American Strategist speaking on behalf of NAMB. I have set a goal of seeing the total number of African-American churches in the SBC increase from 4,000 to 5,000 in the next five years. I am also working with the International Mission Board (IMB), hoping to see the number of African-American missionaries serving around the world increase in the years to come. I have the same three goals today regarding the importance of international missions that I had while I was the convention president: model a personal commitment, educate churches about needs, and instill a vision for the world in the hearts of young people.

My desire is to be faithful to the Lord in every area in which He allows me to lead and to serve. That is also God's desire for you. As you lead the flock that God has entrusted to you, let me again encourage you to be faithful in these seven areas:

1. Be faithful to God.
2. Be faithful to God's Word.
3. Be faithful to your family.
4. Be faithful to the church you are leading.
5. Be faithful through your lifestyle.
6. Be faithful during the good days.
7. Be faithful during the difficult days

Let me remind each of you that *God rewards faithfulness*. As you lead your flock, if you are faithful in the above seven areas, I assure you that God will be faithful to you!

CHAPTER 10

Trusting the True Shepherd

Stephen Rummage

M uch of a shepherd-leader's effectiveness can be determined by answering one simple question: *Is the shepherd worthy of trust?* The late Allan Emery, once president and chief operating officer of the Billy Graham Evangelistic Association, wrote about an evening he spent with a shepherd on the Texas plains. The shepherd, who was tending 2,000 sheep, had built a large fire to keep himself, his guest, and his sheep warm. Sheepdogs slept around the fire as the night grew darker and stars filled the sky.

Suddenly, the quiet prairie scene was interrupted by the distinctive howl of a coyote in the distance, followed by another coyote's answering wail from the opposite direction. The sheepdogs growled as they stared out into the darkness. The sheep, startled from their sleep, groggily reared to their feet and began bleating in fear. The shepherd jumped up and tossed more logs onto the fire, causing the flames to shoot up.

As the fire burned brightly, Emery looked out and saw what appeared to be 4,000 tiny lights in every direction around the campfire. Though puzzled for a moment, he quickly realized the lights were the reflections of the fire in the eyes of the sheep. "In the midst of danger," Emery wrote, "the sheep were not looking out into the darkness, but were keeping their eyes in the direction of their safety, looking toward the shepherd."[1]

Sheep Need Trustworthy Shepherds

Why did the sheep in Emery's story turn to the shepherd? They trusted him. In the church, a similar relationship of trust must connect the flock of God to their shepherd-leader. Sheep need a shepherd they can trust. By nature, they lack direction and easily lose their way. They are vulnerable to attack. They need someone to lead them to water and food. God made sheep that way.

In *Practical Wisdom for Pastors*, Curtis Thomas observed that just as sheep need shepherds to lead them, God has designed His spiritual sheep in the church to need spiritual shepherds to lead them into truth and righteousness. He writes, "Ultimately Jesus is the great Shepherd, but He has chosen men to be His undershepherds to pastor the flock."[2]

Ezekiel 34 is a portrait of contrasting shepherds. Often in the Old Testament, as in many other writings from the ancient Near East, rulers are described as shepherds. Scripture uses shepherd imagery to describe Moses and David in their leadership of Israel (see Isa 63:11; Ps 78:70). Significantly, both men were called to lead God's people when they were working as literal shepherds of actual flocks of sheep. Moses, David, and other shepherds of Israel were more than political or military rulers. The metaphor of a shepherd suggests something deeper than only leadership or governance. Israel's shepherds bore a primary responsibility for the moral and spiritual direction of the nation.[3] At the deepest level, a good shepherd is marked by his care and compassion for the sheep. He actually loves the sheep, and the sheep know they can trust him.

The opening verses of Ezekiel describe false shepherds of Israel, who were neither faithful nor trustworthy. Instead, these leaders abused, misused, misled, exploited, and neglected God's people. The reasons these

---

[1] Allan C. Emery, *A Turtle on a Fencepost: Little Lessons of Large Importance* (Minneapolis: World Wide Publishing Group, 1980), 3.
[2] Curtis C. Thomas, *Practical Wisdom for Pastors: Words of Encouragement and Counsel for a Lifetime of Ministry* (Wheaton, IL: Crossway Books, 2001), 94–95.
[3] Lamar Eugene Cooper, *Ezekiel*, NAC, vol. 17 (Nashville: B&H, 1994), 298.

wicked shepherds could not be trusted are obvious in the text. They were feeding themselves instead of the flock (v. 2). They were butchering the sheep for their own advantage and gain (v. 3). They failed to tend the weak sheep, to care for the injured or sick among their flock, and to search for sheep that were lost (v. 4). They allowed their sheep to become prey for predatory animals (v. 5). As a result of their disloyalty and treachery, God announced His opposition to the false shepherds. He would no longer entrust His sheep to them. Instead, He Himself would rescue His flock (v. 10).

When applied to spiritual leaders in the church, these verses stand as a reminder of how infinitely valuable God's people are to the Lord. Because He loves the sheep so much, God is deeply offended when those who are called to be spiritual shepherds become careless or oppressive in their calling. The passage shows the momentous responsibility borne by a man called to be the spiritual leader of a congregation. Even more, these verses sound a strong warning to pastors against negligence and inattention or, worse yet, self-serving abusiveness as they shepherd God's people. When pastors are more concerned about their own welfare than that of their people, when they use the church as a means of material or professional gain, when they abuse the congregation through false teaching or man-centered leadership, when they are unconcerned about the pain their people are facing, when they fail to restore straying church members through loving discipline, or when they leave their people vulnerable to the attacks and temptations of the enemy, pastors will encounter opposition from the Lord whom they claim to serve. God cannot trust unfaithful shepherds. And neither can His flock.

In contrast to the wicked shepherds, the verses in the last two thirds of Ezekiel 34 describe the Lord's care and provision as the true Shepherd of the sheep of Israel, beginning with this promise: "For this is what the Lord GOD says: See, I Myself will search for My flock and look for them" (Ezek 34:11).

Someone must look after the flock, or the sheep will perish. Because Israel's shepherds have been so deficient and untrustworthy in their duties, God Himself pledges to take on the role of Shepherd to His people. Later in the chapter, God promises that, through the coming Messiah, He will find the straying, rescue the lost, feed the flock, and restore the weak and wounded. "I will establish one shepherd over them—My servant David. He shall feed them and be their shepherd" (Ezek 34:23).

Throughout Ezek 34:11–31, the Lord reveals His own trustworthiness. Pointing forward to Jesus Christ, these verses provide a perfect model for faithful and trustworthy shepherding.

Factors of Trustworthiness

In the pages that follow, four crucial factors that make a shepherd-leader trustworthy will be examined. These factors of trustworthiness are a leader's *intentions,* his *ability,* his *judgment,* and his *character.* In Ezekiel 34, these four aspects of trustworthiness are displayed in the nature of God, with each factor finding its culmination in the person and ministry of Jesus Christ, the good Shepherd. We will conclude by exploring some implications of these four factors of trustworthiness in the leadership of today's pastor-leader.

The Trustworthiness of the Divine Shepherd's Intentions

God can be trusted because of the loving and redemptive intentions He has for His sheep. He expresses these intentions repeatedly in verses 11–16. God intends to search and look for His flock (vv. 11–12); to rescue them (v. 12); to bring them out from the hostile nations, back to their own land (v. 13); to shepherd them in the mountains, valleys, and every inhabited place in their land (v. 13); to lead them to graze in a good pasture (v. 14); to care for them so that they can rest (v. 15); to bring back the lost and straying sheep (v. 16); to bind up the wounds of the injured and strengthen the weak (v. 16); and to destroy those among the flock who have harmed others (v. 16).

The word that most comprehensively expresses the Lord's intention toward His flock is *deliver.* The Lord says that He will "deliver them from all the places where they were scattered on a cloudy and dark day" (Ezek 34:12). The term for "deliver" (Hb. *natsal*) means to snatch someone away from danger or remove someone from harm.[4] The "cloudy and dark day" suggests that God's final deliverance will be the day of the Lord, when God acts in salvation and judgment to establish His righteous kingdom on earth.[5] In Ps 51:14, David uses *natsal* to talk about being rescued from his transgressions: "Deliver me from the guilt of bloodshed, O God, / The God of my salvation, / And my tongue shall sing aloud of Your righteousness." Thus, being rescued by God involves deliverance from sin's guilt and also being snatched away from the coming judgment of God upon the sinful world.

God ultimately accomplished His redemptive intention by sending the Messiah. The image of a shepherd looking for the stray and then risking his own safety in order to rescue the sheep foreshadows Jesus's kingdom parable of the Lost Sheep, a parable that Jesus likely told in light of Ezekiel 34:

> What man of you, having a hundred sheep, if he loses one of them, does not leave the ninety-nine in the wilderness, and go after the one which is lost until he finds it? And when he has found it, he lays it on his shoulders, rejoicing. And when he comes home, he calls together his friends and neighbors, saying to them, "Rejoice with me, for I have found my sheep which was lost!" (Luke 15:4–6)

Jesus used shepherd imagery to speak of His saving intentions. He told His disciples, "[T]he Son of Man has come to seek and to save that which was lost" (Luke 19:10) and, "The good shepherd gives His life for the sheep" (John 10:11).

The Lord's intentions for His flock are trustworthy. He never intends evil for His people. He only intends the very best. Through Jesus Christ, God overwhelmingly and preeminently intends to rescue His people and restore them into the fullness of His blessing. And, as we will see in the next section, because God's ability is as trustworthy as His intentions are,

---

[4] Joel T. Hamme, "Salvation," in *Lexham Theological Wordbook*, ed. Douglas Mangum, Derek R. Brown, Rachel Klippenstein, and Rebekah Hurst (Bellingham, WA: Lexham Press, 2014).

[5] John B. Taylor, *Ezekiel: An Introduction and Commentary*, Tyndale Old Testament Commentaries, vol. 22 (Downers Grove, IL: InterVarsity Press, 1969), 215.

His sheep can be assured that their divine Shepherd's good intentions will come to fruition.

The Trustworthiness of the Divine Shepherd's Ability

God's undefeatable ability is such that His plans will not fail. Indeed, God's wonderful intentions for His people would leave them disappointed and disillusioned if His plans were not undergirded by His power and ability to accomplish what He intends. Lamar Cooper observes that Ezek 34:11–29 overflows with first-person promises from God. For a total of 29 times in these verses, God emphatically declares, "I will." Each repeated, "I will" underscores the indefatigability of God to do what He intends to do. Cooper notes: "The proliferation of 'I wills' in 34:10–29 suggests Yahweh's determination personally to be involved in the lives and destinies of his people."[6]

God's unstoppable power gives hope to His people as they trust in Him. The trustworthiness of God's ability is revealed throughout Scripture. God asked Abraham and Sarah, "Is anything too hard for the LORD?" (Gen 18:14). Job testified before God, "I know that You can do everything, / And that no purpose of Yours can be withheld from You" (Job 42:2). Psalm 115:3 declares, "But our God is in heaven; / He does whatever He pleases." The prophet Jeremiah proclaims, "Oh, Lord GOD! Behold, You have made the heavens and earth by Your great power and outstretched arm. There is nothing too hard for You" (Jer 32:17). Jesus told his disciples, "The things which are impossible with men are possible with God" (Luke 18:27).

The ability of God's power to elicit trust is illustrated powerfully in Exodus as the people of Israel crossed the Red Sea. The people were like sheep, being physically herded and moved along by their human shepherd, Moses, as he followed the commands of the Lord to bring them out of Egypt. At the close of the Red Sea account, Exod 14:31 records: "Thus Israel saw the great work which the LORD had done in Egypt; so the people feared the LORD, and believed the LORD and His servant Moses." Seeing how God had delivered the Israelites at the Red Sea and drowned the

---

[6] Cooper, *Ezekiel*, 301.

pursuing Egyptians, the people were moved both to fear and believe God and to trust Moses as their human leader because of God's supernatural ability.

To an even greater extent, the cross and resurrection of Jesus Christ bring assurance of the power of God to accomplish His purposes. The trustworthiness of God's ability reaches both its height and depth in the work of Jesus. Second Corinthians 1:20 affirms, "For all the promises of God in Him are Yes, and in Him Amen, to the glory of God through us." Each "I will" of God finds its culmination in Christ, proving the trustworthiness of the Lord's power.

The Trustworthiness of the Divine Shepherd's Judgment

At the end of Ezek 34:16, God promises, "I will . . . feed them in judgment." The Hebrew term for "judgment" (*mishpat*) indicates decisions and actions that flow from wisdom and righteousness.[7] The text goes on to reveal that God's judgment is sure, so that He can distinguish His true sheep from those who are not His sheep. God promises to exercise a discerning type of judgment among His flock: in verses 17, 20, and 22:

- "And as for you, O My flock, thus says the Lord GOD: 'Behold, I shall judge between sheep and sheep, between rams and goats'" (v. 17).
- "Therefore thus says the Lord GOD to them: 'Behold, I Myself will judge between the fat and the lean sheep'" (v. 20).
- "[T]herefore I will save My flock, and they shall no longer be a prey; And I will judge between sheep and sheep" (v. 22).

In his commentary on Ezekiel, John Taylor notes that flocks in biblical times usually consisted of a mixture of both sheep and goats. The Hebrew word *seh* in verses 17, 20, and 22—translated "sheep" in many English Bibles—simply meant a "member of the flock," whether a sheep or a goat. Taylor writes:

---

[7] William L. Holladay, ed., *A Concise Hebrew and Aramaic Lexicon of the Old Testament* (Leiden: Brill; Grand Rapids: Eerdmans, 1988), s.v. "מִשְׁפָּט."

Ezekiel is saying that the powerful and prosperous citizens, who had been greedily taking for themselves all the good things of the land and denying the benefit of them to their fellows, were going to be judged by the Shepherd. The flock will in fact be purified, not only of its bad leadership but also of its bad members.[8]

As the true Shepherd of Israel, God will identify the wicked members of the flock based on their conduct. The wicked are those in the flock who follow the leadership of the wicked shepherds, taking advantage of the weak and oppressing them. The wicked in the flock not only eat greedily from the best part of the pasture, but they also trample down the rest of the field and ruin it. They muddy the drinking waters so that the weaker members of the flock are not able to get nourishment (Ezek 34:18–19). The wicked also harass and harm the weaker members. Verse 21 depicts them butting the weak ones with their horns to drive them away. In His righteous judgment and perfect wisdom, God will not allow these wicked practices to continue. He will judge between one sheep and another.

God's promise to separate righteous sheep from wicked goats finds it fullest expression in the judging work of Jesus Christ. In the future, before the beginning of His millennial reign, Jesus will separate sheep from goats (Matt 25:32–33):

All the nations will be gathered before Him, and He will separate them one from another, as a shepherd divides sheep from the goats. And He will set the sheep on His right hand, but the goats on the left.

As in Ezekiel, the factor that will differentiate the wicked goats from the righteous sheep in the flock will be what the members of the flock did or failed to do. Those in the flock who showed compassion to the hungry, the thirsty, the stranger, the naked, the sick, and the imprisoned will be judged and rewarded as sheep (vv. 34–40). Those who failed to show compassion will be judged and condemned as goats (vv. 41–45). So, the Lord's trustworthiness as a shepherd is evidenced in His ability to differentiate

---

[8] Taylor, *Ezekiel: An Introduction and Commentary*, 216.

the righteous from the wicked and to reward and punish in a way that is completely just, based on His righteous judgment.

Another aspect of God's trustworthy judgment is revealed in Ezekiel 34. By His judgment and perfect wisdom, the Lord is also able to determine what His sheep truly need. The "covenant of peace" described in verses 25–31 shows how the Lord wisely discerns and meets the needs of His people. With insight that comes from knowing His sheep intimately, God, as the perfect shepherd-leader, provides the flock's deepest yearnings. Included in the Lord's covenant of peace are promises to send Israel "showers of blessing" (v. 26), security (v. 27), freedom from fear (v. 28), a place of abundance rather than famine (v. 29), deliverance from the taunts of their enemies (v. 29), God's divine presence (v.30), and knowledge that they are God's people (v. 30).

The "covenant of peace" in Ezekiel reflects the Lord's judgment to discern and provide exactly what His flock needs. This aspect of God's character is perhaps most poignantly summarized in the opening words of David's shepherd psalm: "The LORD is my shepherd; / I shall not want" (Ps 23:1). As the church's true Shepherd, Jesus Christ has perfect knowledge of the greatest need of His sheep. Jesus says, "My sheep hear My voice, and I know them, and they follow Me. And I give them eternal life, and they shall never perish; neither shall anyone snatch them out of My hand" (John 10:27–28). Because the Lord avenges wickedness, rewards righteousness, and provides for His people, ultimately giving them eternal life, God's judgment can be trusted.

The Trustworthiness of the Divine Shepherd's Character

The Lord's divine character is unassailable. He can be trusted to do only that which is righteous and good. As noted throughout this discussion, Ezekiel's description of the divine Shepherd of God's people was fulfilled in the coming of Jesus Christ. The coming Shepherd, identified by God as "my servant David" (v. 23), would be altogether unlike the wicked rulers who had served with selfish motivations. Instead, God was promising to send a shepherd like David, whose character reflected God's own heart (1 Sam 13:14). Cooper writes: "The hope of the Messiah soared with God's promise of 'one shepherd' (Ezek 34:23) who would regather the people and reinstate the line of David to bring people to a personal knowledge of God."[9]

In John 10, a passage closely related to Ezekiel 34, Jesus describes Himself as "the good shepherd." The Greek word for "good" (*kalos*) describes that which is noble, wholesome, and beautiful, in contrast with that which is wicked, mean, foul, and unlovely. Jesus's innate goodness is what moved Him to sacrifice Himself on the cross.[10] This type of perfect, sacrificial goodness makes Jesus unique in character. By calling Himself "the good shepherd," Jesus is magnifying His own character as one who sacrificially protects, guides, and nurtures His flock.

James Boice notes that Jesus is represented as a shepherd three times in the New Testament and that each time the word "shepherd" is described with a different adjective to highlight a different aspect of the Lord's character. In John 10, Jesus is the "good" Shepherd, who lays down His life for the sheep (John 10:11). In Heb 13:20–21, Jesus is represented as the "great" Shepherd: "Now may the God of peace who brought up our Lord Jesus from the dead, that great Shepherd of the sheep, through the blood of the everlasting covenant, make you complete in every good work to do His will." Here, the emphasis is on the Shepherd's ability to accomplish His work through His sheep. In 1 Pet 5:4, Jesus is called "the Chief Shepherd": "[A]nd when the Chief Shepherd appears, you will receive the crown of glory that does not fade away." This image points to the reward that Jesus brings to those who serve Him at His return. Boice concludes:

> These passages highlight the focal points of Christ's ministry. As the Good Shepherd, Christ dies for the sheep. As the Great Shepherd, Christ rises from the dead so that He might serve the sheep. As the Chief Shepherd, Christ returns to reward those who have been faithful in the responsibilities to which they have been assigned as under-shepherds.[11]

---

[9] Cooper, *Ezekiel*, 306.

[10] Joachim Wanke, "καλός," in *Exegetical Dictionary of the New Testament*, ed. Horst Robert Balz and Gerhard Schneider, (Grand Rapids: Eerdmans, 1990), 2:244–45.

[11] James Montgomery Boice, *Genesis: An Expositional Commentary* (Grand Rapids: Baker Books, 1998), 1165.

In every case, Jesus Christ, the good, great, and Chief Shepherd has a character that is completely trustworthy.

The Rod and the Staff: Being a Trustworthy Shepherd

Understanding that God is trustworthy in every aspect—His intentions, His ability, His judgment, and His character—provides a high standard for shepherd-leaders in the church today. Moreover, knowing that Jesus, the Chief Shepherd, will return to reward those who are faithful in serving Him, requires those of us in pastoral ministry to emulate His trustworthiness as we serve His people.

Remember the simple question that shapes the effectiveness of any ministry: *Is the shepherd worthy of trust?* With that central question in mind, pastors would be well served to examine their own hearts and ministries with four other related "trust" questions:

Can my intentions be trusted?
Can my ability be trusted?
Can my judgment be trusted?
Can my character be trusted?

In the final part of this chapter, some of the pieces of the pastoral puzzle that must be in place in your life for you to answer each of these questions affirmatively will be contemplated.

Leading with Trustworthy Intentions

In 1933, as Nazi Germany entered the fullness of its power and many German Christians seemed too frightened, impotent, or unconcerned to oppose Adolf Hitler's evil, pastor Dietrich Bonhoeffer fled Germany in disgust and discouragement. Rather than staying in his homeland, Bonhoeffer left to become the pastor of a German-speaking congregation in England. Karl Barth wrote a pointed letter to his dispirited colleague, part of which read:

What is all this about "going away," and "quietness of pastoral work," etc., at a moment when you are wanted in Germany? You,

who know as well as I do that the opposition in Berlin and the opposition of the church in Germany as a whole stands inwardly on
such weak feet! . . . Why aren't you always there where so much
could depend on there being a couple of game people on the watch
at every occasion, great or small, and trying to save what there is
to be saved? . . .

***

I think that I can see from your letter that you, like all of us—yes,
all of us!—are suffering under the quite common difficulty of taking "certain steps" in the present chaos. But should it not dawn
on you that there is no reason for withdrawing from this chaos,
that we are rather required in and with our uncertainty, even if
we should stumble or go wrong 10 times or 100 times, to do our
bit . . .

***

One simply cannot become weary now. Still less can one go to
England! What in all the world would you want to do there? . . . You
must now leave go of all these intellectual flourishes and special
considerations, however interesting they may be, and think of only
one thing, that you are a German, that the house of your church is
on fire, that you know enough to be able to help and that you must
return to your post by the next ship.[12]

Bonhoeffer returned to Germany 16 months later, eventually to be exe-
cuted for his opposition to the Third Reich. Barth, even with the shortcom-
ings of his neoorthodox theology, expressed a clear understanding of what
a pastor's intentions should be: to stay on the line in the face of danger,
caring for God's flock.

Jesus said that having trustworthy intentions is a distinguishing
mark of a true shepherd. He contrasted these intentions to the wavering

---

[12] Dietrich Bonhoeffer, "Karl Barth," *Christian History Magazine, Issue 65: Ten Influential Christians of the 20th Century* (Carol Stream, IL: Christianity Today, 2000), 25.

commitment of a hired man, who abandons the sheep in times of distress: "The hired man, since he is not the shepherd and doesn't own the sheep, leaves them and runs away when he sees a wolf coming. The wolf then snatches and scatters them. This happens because he is a hired man and doesn't care about the sheep" (John 10:12–13). A shepherd cares about the sheep in a way the hireling never can. Steven Smith has astutely observed that pastors are called to imitate Christ "in His selfless deference to sinful people above His own desires."[13] Just as Jesus cares for the sheep so much that he would never abandon them, a trustworthy undershepherd will genuinely care for the Lord's sheep with sacrificial, longsuffering intentions.

A pastor with trustworthy intentions will not abandon the flock to which God has called him solely for another position of perceived greater prominence, ease, or income. He will stay or go only at God's bidding. He will preach the Word of God faithfully, accurately, and completely, even when doing so harms his own personal popularity or offends people of influence. He will freely give himself to provide spiritual care for and nurture the sheep. He will sacrifice his own preferences, his own comfort, and even his own personal safety, for the sake of faithfulness to the flock entrusted to him.

Leading with Trustworthy Ability

A trustworthy shepherd-leader serves the Lord and His people with skill and excellence. He will seek to give his very best efforts to studying the biblical text and preparing messages to preach each week; providing for pastoral care, counseling, and guidance for the flock; showing love and compassion for those who are hurting, ill, or bereaved; and attending to the administrative details of overseeing a church's varied ministries. To these ends, the pastor will seek to train himself for fruitful work and to delegate and find competent leaders to help in the areas where he is weak.

Having done all of those things, pastors must beware of the danger of serving the church in their own strength or from their own skillfulness. When a young pastor begins his journey in ministry, he is often struck by

---

[13] Steven W. Smith, *Dying to Preach: Embracing the Cross in the Pulpit* (Grand Rapids: Kregel, 2009), 61.

his own inadequacy and forced to his knees in prayerful reliance on God's strength. Later in the journey, he can be fooled into thinking that human ability can substitute for divine empowerment.

I remember driving down the long rural highway that led to my first church. Someone has since told me that, no matter what size it is, your first church always seems like a megachurch. That was certainly true for me. Though the congregation was small—perhaps 60 or 80 people on a good Sunday—and though the pastoral leadership responsibilities were very limited, I drove up to that church and prayed, "Lord, I can't do this. I need your help." As I prepared to preach each Sunday, as I tried to lead in meetings, as I walked into hospital rooms and encountered crisis situations over those first years of ministry, I prayed that prayer silently and out loud many times over: "Lord, I can't do this. I need your help."

More than 20 years later, I have thousands of sermons under my belt and in my file cabinets, I've led more meetings of staff and laypeople than I can number, and I've run into just about every crisis scenario imaginable in pastoral care. As a result, I face the danger of saying:

> I can do an exegetical study of a passage of Scripture on my own. I can illustrate and apply the text in my sermon. I know how to do that. I've been trained to do that. I know what to say when I go into this emergency room because I've said similar words before in similar circumstance. I know how to deal with this question or this issue in this meeting. It's territory I've traveled many times.

But, if I start to say and think those kinds of things, I'm in an extremely dangerous position. While education, training, and experience can increase a pastor's ability, no man ever gets past the place where he needs to cry out constantly, "Lord, I can't do this. I need you." In the upper room, Jesus was talking to His most trusted people, future shepherds of His flock who had the benefit of personal training and experience under the tutelage of the Lord Himself. Jesus told the disciples, "I am the vine, you are the branches. He who abides in Me, and I in him, bears much fruit; for without Me you can do nothing" (John 15:5). Without abiding in Jesus, absolutely nothing of eternal significance can be accomplished in any arena of life. Certainly in ministry, only constant connection to Christ can produce spiritual fruit. Our ability as shepherd-leaders flows from abiding in Jesus. While "abiding" has a wide number of implications and expressions in the life of a Christ-follower, its core involves trusting in Christ daily and seeking the filling of the Holy Spirit. Al Mohler writes, "The absence of a conscious dependence upon the Holy Spirit is a sign that the preacher does not understand his task and calling."[14] Through conscious and deliberate reliance upon the Lord Jesus and the power of His Spirit, shepherd-leaders can serve with trustworthy ability.

Leading with Trustworthy Judgment

A pastor can think of his judgment in terms of both its fruit and its root. The fruit of godly judgment is Christ-honoring, disciple-growing, and church-nourishing decisions. *Christ-honoring* decisions are choices that reflect God's holiness, result in the gospel of Jesus being propagated, are consistent with the Word of God, and advance God's kingdom. *Disciple-growing* decisions are those that help members of the flock become more like Christ, engaging them in ministry, service, and the pursuit of a godly lifestyle. *Church-nourishing* decisions take the congregation in the right direction corporately. These choices can include starting new ministry initiatives, buying property, building, making staffing decisions, altering existing ministry programs, and other similar decisions. When a pastor has trustworthy judgment, he will seek to make choices that follow God's best purposes.

The root of godly judgment is God's wisdom, which the Lord gives to those who seek His wisdom, obey His Word, and fear Him. Several well-known passages of Scripture speak clearly about how we gain wisdom. Leaders gain wisdom from the Word of God. We are instructed to let God's Word dwell in us "richly in all wisdom, teaching and admonishing one another" (Col 3:16). We also gain wisdom as a gift of God. According to Jas 1:5, anyone who lacks wisdom should ask God, "who gives to all liberally and without reproach, and it will be given to him." For the shepherd-leader, as for any follower of Jesus Christ, God makes His wisdom available when

---

[14] R. Albert Mohler, Jr., *He is not Silent: Preaching in a Postmodern World* (Chicago: Moody, 2008), 45.

we recognize we need it and simply ask Him for it in faith. Ultimately, wisdom comes through the fear of God. Ps 111:10 says, "The fear of the LORD is the beginning of wisdom; / A good understanding have all those who do His commandments." When shepherd-leaders have a proper understanding of who God is, when we revere His power and authority, and when we fear displeasing Him or dishonoring His name—that is the beginning place for wise decisions and sound judgment.

In practical terms, the pastor's first year serving a new congregation can be instrumental in establishing the foundation for making good decisions. The early days of a pastor's ministry at a church have often been called the "honeymoon" period. During those beginning days, weeks, or months of a pastorate, every sermon the pastor preaches seems wonderful and every decision he makes appears wise in the eyes of the people. More realistically, these early halcyon days in a new ministry are really a time of suspended judgment, when the congregation is assessing the trustworthiness of the pastor.

To create maximum trust during that time, a smart pastor will seek to learn his flock before plunging headlong into decisions that he may later regret. After all, he is still discovering how the people of the congregation think about themselves, worship, handle church finances, minister, and approach other aspects of church life. Concerning the first year of a pastorate, Robert Kemper offers this wise counsel:

> While I'm freshly exposed to a new church culture, I actively take mental, and some literal, notes on the congregation. I've always found this type of listening a highly active process for me. I try to be present at everything; I skip nothing. I need to be seen much more than heard, partly because I don't want to stick my foot in my mouth more than necessary![15]

Pastors would do well to learn a lesson from the mother who asked her pediatrician, "How can I keep the confidence of my child?" The doctor

---

[15] Robert Kemper, "The First Year," in *Mastering Transitions* by Ed Bratcher, Robert Kemper, and Douglas Scott, Mastering Ministry Series (Portland, OR: Multnomah, 1991), 82.

replied, "Never lose it." Our congregations want to trust us.[16] By patiently seeking the Lord's direction, depending on Him through prayer, and seeking His Word for counsel, a shepherd-leader can honor the Lord and then bless his congregation with trustworthy judgment and wise decisions.

Leading with Trustworthy Character

Psalm 78:72 offers this assessment of David as a leader of Israel: "So he shepherded them according to the integrity of his heart / And guided them by the skillfulness of his hands." While David's skill as a shepherd was important, his purity was essential. Look back at the description of the false shepherds of Israel in Ezek 34:1–10. Their main problem was not that they were unskilled or simply made bad decisions, though both of those things may have been true. Their primary failing was moral and spiritual. They were corrupt. They were wicked. Their hearts were not pure.

One of my mentors in ministry was a man who became the executive pastor of a large congregation after having served a career as a top executive with a telecommunications company. He told me once, "I've seen a man lose hundreds and even thousands of dollars for the phone company because of a bad decision, and yet keep his job. On the other hand, I've seen a man get fired because he stole quarters out of a pay phone." The lesson is clear—errors of skill and judgment can be overcome. Errors of character are much more detrimental. A. W. Tozer expressed his commitment to character and integrity this way: "I expect to so live and so preach that people can bring their friends to my church and assure them they can believe what they hear from my pulpit. I may be wrong sometimes, but I want always to be honest."[17]

Without diligently guarding our own character and examining our integrity on a regular basis, shepherd-leaders with the best intentions can fall morally and spiritually, wounding themselves, their families, the church, and the kingdom of God in the process. Even King David, a man after

---

[16] Warren W. Wiersbe and David Wiersbe, *The Elements of Preaching: The Art of Biblical Preaching Clearly and Simply Presented* (Wheaton, IL: Tyndale, 1986), 98–99.

[17] A. W. Tozer, in *The Tozer Topical Reader*, comp. Ron Eggert, vol. 2 (Camp Hill, PA: WingSpread, 1998), 71.

God's own heart, found himself in deep sin when he failed to guard his eyes and his actions. I suggest that pastors regularly ask themselves a number of questions about their character:

- Do I tell the truth privately and publicly, without exaggeration?
- Do I keep confidences?
- Do I give credit when I use the words and ideas of others in my preaching and writing?
- Do I seek to keep the promises I make? And do I seek forgiveness when I am unable to keep a promise?
- Do I guard my relationships and dealings with the opposite sex, carefully establishing boundaries to keep me from temptation or reproach?
- Am I honest with monetary resources, watching over my financial dealings so that no charge of dishonesty, misappropriation, or conflict of interest could be credibly brought against my congregation, my family, or me?
- Do I honor the Lord by giving Him tithes and offerings?
- Am I consistently spending time in prayer, personally studying God's Word, and sharing the gospel of Christ with others?
- Am I the same person with my wife and my family, by myself, and before God that I portray myself to be in the pulpit and before my people?

Questions like these can be a good starting place for a shepherd-leader who desires to guard the purity of his own heart.[18]

Writing in the sixth century, Gregory the Great observed:

> The pastor should always be pure in thought . . . no impurity ought to pollute him who has undertaken the office of wiping away the stains in the hearts of others . . . for the hand that would cleanse

---

[18] Recently, the National Association of Evangelicals adopted a code of ethics for pastors that may be helpful. It can be accessed at http://nae.net/wp–content/uploads/2012/06 /Code–of–Ethics–for–Pastors1.pdf.

from dirt must be clean, lest, being itself sordid with clinging mire, it soil whatever it touches all the more.[19]

A trustworthy shepherd-leader is one whose spiritual and moral character reflects the holiness and righteousness of Jesus.

Conclusion

The truth bears repeating: sheep need trustworthy shepherds. So many of the leaders to whom people turn—whether in politics, education, or the culture at large—have proven to be untrustworthy and harmful to those they lead. Sadly, too many pastors have abused trust in some way, dishonored the Lord Jesus, and exploited and harmed the flock. However, undershepherds can prove themselves trustworthy in their ability, their intentions, their judgment, and their character as they look to the great Shepherd, who excels in every way and empowers the pastor to shepherd His sheep faithfully.

---

[19] Jay Kesler, *Being Holy, Being Human: Dealing with the Expectations of Ministry*, The Leadership Library 13 (Carol Stream, IL: Christianity Today, Inc., 1988), 13.

Name Index

Subject Index

Scripture Index